UNLEASH YOUR LADY BOSS

STEFANIE PETERS

ISBN 13: 978-1-945769-18-4
eISBN: 978-1-945769-19-1

Library of Congress Catalog Number: 2016954399

Printed in the United States of America
First Printing: 2016

20   19   18   17   16   5   4   3   2   1

Cover design by Nupoor Gordon
Interior design by Kim Morehead

Published by W.I. Creative Publishing, an imprint of Wise Ink Creative Publishing.

W.J ★CREATIVE★
PUBLISHING

W.I. Creative Publishing
837 Glenwood Avenue
wiseinkpub.com

To order, visit seattlebookcompany.com or call (734)426-6248.
Reseller discounts available.

CONTENTS

✦ ——————— ✦

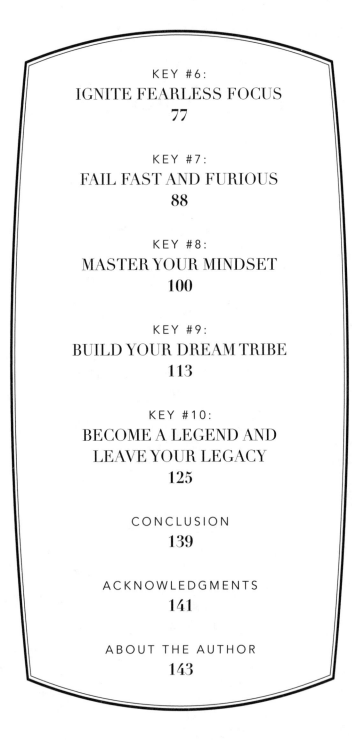

INTRODUCTION

Ten thousand people are cheering for me. I am being interviewed by the CEO of a billion-dollar company. Holy wow—I'm a twenty-two-year-old blonde gal who just shattered the glass ceiling. I'm pretty sure more adrenaline has shot through my body in the last ten minutes than in the last ten months. I'm humbled and jazzed beyond belief to have led my team to break *the* record of *all time*. The Inc. 500 company awards me an honor few will ever receive. I literally pinch myself. Though I'm extremely nervous, I decide to embrace the moment and power through.

Under the hot stage lights and television cameras, and in front of thousands of trailblazers, my CEO declares with pride and amazement, "Stefanie, you're the youngest female executive director in the twenty-five-year history of the company. You've created enough residual income that, by retirement age, you'll have earned six-point-four million dollars. I know what a hard worker you are, and you're growing like crazy, so I know you won't stop here. You will actually earn millions more. Congratulations. You've paved the way for countless people, inspired the masses, and led from the heart. You're my hero!"

That moment changed my life forever. I knew it was my time. But I didn't know I was destined to lead a movement.

So if you want to change your life and become a woman on a mission, you're reading the right book. If you feel there has to be more to life, take heart. If you're committed to being the boss of your future, grab your stilettos, kick those fears to the curb, and let's get after it, sister! You're on the brink of your breakthrough.

I, like you, knew there must be more to life. I realized that just having a job, doing the same thing day after day, and being stuck in a rut wasn't for me. I knew in my heart that my life was destined for more! I never wanted to work for forty years, sixty hours a week, and retire with 40 percent of the income that most people can't live on in the first place. Nor did I want to be one of the unlucky folks who gets laid off, their territory cut, downsized, outsized, or flat-out fired. The 40/60/40 club just wasn't my deal. My inner Lady Boss was on fire and I didn't want to settle for a life short of dazzling.

I started to envision the fabulous future I believed God had planned for me (more on this in Key #1). So I chose faith over fear and embraced it all. It was time to go all in and fiercely sashay into the heart and hustle of my purpose. When you know you're living below your potential, it's time to step up to the plate, put on your big-girl pants, and get to work.

I want to challenge you.

Don't take the plan everyone says you're **supposed** *to follow. Instead, choose the greater purpose* **destined** *for you.*

But let's get real. There's a major thing in your way: it's called *life*. Your to-do list always seems to grow no matter how much work you do. Not to mention you have responsibilities: a job; bills; relationships; dinners to prepare; and calls, texts, and e-mails to send. And when you finally have a break from the to-do list, there are other distractions like Facebook, Instagram, Twitter, and that blowout sale with your name on it.

9

On top of everything else, there are those fears that get in your way *every time*. What if you fail, right? What if people think you're freaking nuts for pursuing your juicy, life-inspiring goals? If you're like many, you've convinced yourself that though your nine-to-five isn't fabulous, at least it pays the bills. After all, you should be thankful you even have a job, right?

Yes, be thankful, but don't think you have to settle. Know that if you're looking for more, it's out there, and you can indeed create it if you're willing to work for it.

I want to challenge you to dream big and build your own empire. Because if you don't, someone else will hire you to build theirs. And be honest: you're reading this book because you want to be fabulously in love with your life. You want to make an impact, change the world, and hang out with people you actually like. What's more, you crave a future that harbors no regrets. Stop hitting that repeat button. I know you can be the courageous, empowering Lady Boss you long to be. Girlfriend, it's time to stop living by default. You're at the right place, at the right time, to create your life by design.

Possibilities are in front of you. You don't have to go find them. Your opportunities are flashing bright neon lights (dare I say hot pink?), begging to be noticed, screaming for your uninterrupted attention. But you're too busy to look up. Stop ignoring the signs and go achieve your greatness!

I want you to throw out all notions that the road ahead is easy. Do that now. Let it go. When you board the journey to intentional living, it's a freaking workout. Investing in yourself is no walk in the park. Your fabulous life requires working hard, stomping your doubts into oblivion, and shaking off fear as you unleash your Lady Boss.

If this were easy, *every* woman would do it. I repeat: if this were easy, every woman would be the boss of her life. But for those of us who do make the decision to live our lives on our own terms, we have to get comfortable with three facts. First, there is no such thing as comfortable. You'll have to challenge yourself every day to keep reaching for the greatness that is in you. Second, you'll make people uncomfortable. When you reveal your true light to the world, people may accuse you of dreaming too big. If this happens, send them grace; they haven't yet discovered their own true light. Keep your head up, hold the sparkle in your eyes, and run *your* race. And third, when you ignite your Lady Boss light, it will illuminate your dreams and impact the world at large. And the best part is that you'll bring others with you on this fabulous journey.

If you're like me, you've read countless self-help books, taken empowerment courses, or at the very least read soul-affirming blogs and articles searching for "the answer." I spent years doing just that until I'd either get lost, give up, or talk myself out of the suggested process. I need things simple. I also need things fun and doable. This Lady Boss doesn't like complicated.

The principles in this book have worked for me and for the hundreds of clients I've coached through the years. When I was unleashing my Lady Boss, I needed solutions that could be applied immediately and that actually worked in real time. Call me impatient, but life waits for no one. Life especially doesn't wait for the woman with the "can I really do this?" complex or the woman with shiny-object syndrome. By the way, I wrote this book for that woman. I was that woman. But I learned the fundamental keys to unlock the life I've always wanted. And now, thanks to the principles in this book, my clients are experiencing freedom, fulfilling their purpose, and having a blast every step of the way—glitz, glamour, and all.

I started this process at age eighteen by learning the ten Lady Boss Keys. I paid cash for my college education and my first car. I bought my first house at nineteen and burned that mortgage by age twenty-three. I'm positively jazzed by the life I've designed.

A great friend and student of these success principles says, "Since applying these fundamentals, I now have a thriving business, was crowned Mrs. Minnesota United States, feel balance in my life, and truly am living the good ole American dream . . . working hard, playing hard, enjoying my family, and living on purpose!"

I promise that if you follow the how-to guide in this book, you'll be able to play a bigger game, break through your mental barriers, leverage your time as a busy professional, and fulfill your purpose without compromising your paycheck.

My balls-to-the-wall challenge to you: Don't be the woman who misses opportunities because of fear, or worse, because you doubt your greatness. And don't get sucked into the white noise of mediocrity and live far below your potential. You're better than that. You're phenomenal, and from one Lady Boss to another, I know you're ready to take action and craft your own life story. This is your time to rise up, step out on faith, and live your dream.

My philosophy goes hand in hand with Calamity Jane, who declared, "I figure, if a girl wants to be a legend, she should go ahead and be one!"

Your dreams are possible, even while working a full-time job, but only if you have the courage to believe in *you*.

STEFANIE PETERS

My goal is to empower you to live life by design—not default.

And trust me, I take my goals seriously. I'll run around the world with you, but I won't walk across the street without you! This is a team effort. Are you game? If you're sick and tired of being sick and tired and you're ready to unleash your Lady Boss, buckle up, sister. You're in for the ride of your life. #LADYBOSSFORLIFE #GameOn.

ENVISION YOUR ULTIMATE LADY BOSS LIFE

#LifeByDesign

"Create the highest, grandest vision possible for your life, because you become what you believe."

— Oprah Winfrey

First off, let's get something straight: You're a rock star! The mere fact that you're alive at *this* moment on *this* planet isn't a coincidence. Think about it: scientists estimate that your being born was a one in four hundred trillion chance. Lady Boss, you've been given an unbelievable lifetime opportunity to leave your mark. Period. End of story.

So What Is a Lady Boss?

A woman who shines her light to the world through actively pursuing her God-given potential. She knows when to throw punches and when to roll with them. She never allows others to determine her destiny. She feels the fear, confronts it, and grabs the pen to write her own story. She pursues her purpose to inspire and empower others to unleash their greatness within.

If you don't see life as one big opportunity, you're going to miss your blessings. When I stop and think about all that I can do every day to make my moments count, it sends chills down my spine. Living on autopilot is a killer for the Lady Boss. It saddens me to see so many walking through life like zombies, settling for average. I've seen countless talented and gifted women with amazing potential succumb to their own fears, indecision, and lack of belief.

The problem is that it's so flippin' easy to settle, get crazy tired, make it halfway to a dream, and quit in frustration. Trust me, I've been there. (During the first six months of my career, I was going nowhere really fast.)

We all have haters and doubters at every turn trying to dictate the trajectory of our God-given lives. I'm here to tell you that doubting your doubters takes practice (especially when you're your biggest doubter). Further, when you're at your weakest is when you'll often have to fight the hardest. It's always darkest just before dawn. But I have a few secrets that will cut autopilot living off right at the knees.

First, you've got to realize that you have everything within you to accomplish your God-given purpose. That's right— you don't have to buy anything or recite magic words to un-

15

lock some secret door. You're phenomenal. Own it. The most powerful step you can take right now to unleash your Lady Boss within is to make the intentional decision to shift your mindset. From this day forward, you will claim your position as a Lady Boss. No more wavering back and forth. And because this is the first step on your new road to building your empire, I want this commitment sealed and signed, sister!

Next, I want you to activate your vision. Your dream is no longer just a hope or a pie-in-the-sky desire anymore. It's real, Lady Boss. So repeat after me: "I am phenomenal, and I am officially ready to crush it."

Glad we got that out of the way.

Now that you've owned your inner Lady Boss, it's time for some fun. I love this quote from sportscaster Stuart Scott:

"Don't downgrade your dream just to fit your reality. Upgrade your conviction to match your destiny."

—Stuart Scott

What did you dream about when you were five years old? Life was exciting, the world was bright, and the doubters hadn't told you that you couldn't accomplish the "impossible." Do you remember what the limitless possibilities looked like before "reality" kicked in?

Lady Boss Life Hack:
Don't Fall into the Someday Trap

*If you've always wanted to travel or go on an exotic trip to Bali, pack your suitcase, create the itinerary, and start planning how to make it happen. If you've always wanted to start your own business, it's time to buy the domain name for your website. If you want to write a book, it's time to see that book in your hands, published, and making its impact. Write your first chapter, or even the first paragraph! If you want to launch a blog, imagine that blog live and in color doing its thing and being shared by millions of engaged followers! Write your first post by the end of this week. Don't wait. The word **dream** is a verb; dreams are not meant to be stagnant ideas in your brilliant brain, girlfriend.*

17

CALL YOUR DREAMS TO LIFE

Start reviewing your list of "dreams." What have you always wanted to do in this life? Where do you ultimately want your Lady Boss life to take you? From now on, explore each dream with a decided belief that it can happen. Sure, you might decide to move on to something else. After all, Lady Bosses overflow with ideas and dreams. Ideas come at us from all angles all day long. We're creative geniuses. You certainly don't have to pursue every idea. But you do need to believe they're *all* possible. Every. Single. One.

I'm crazy about the way well-known entrepreneur, author, and motivational speaker Jim Rohn put it:

*"If you don't design your own life
plan, chances are you'll fall into someone
else's plan. And guess what they have
planned for you? Not much."*

That's why it's not enough to *know* you're destined for greatness. You have to design your master life plan on purpose. To call your dreams to life, you have to visualize what your life looks like at its absolute best. Before you go to bed tonight, I want you to spend time dreaming while awake. Close your eyes if it helps. What do you see? What does your big, juicy Lady Boss life look like? What are you wearing? Where do you live? What makes it vibrant, colorful, and out of this world?

KICK OUT YOUR BAGGAGE

If you're like most people, you've probably been handed some pretty challenging stuff in life! I get it. But why not take the cards you've been dealt and light up the world in a major way? After all, your life can be big, bold, and lush. What are the outrageous and epic steps you can take to make that happen? Do you have baggage you need to kick to the curb? The secret to envisioning your ultimate Lady Boss life is designing possibilities. Dream ideas so powerful that they'll propel you to the next level. Your baggage isn't invited on your journey to greatness.

To kick your baggage out of the dream, you need to acknowledge it. Whose voices do you hear saying you're not good enough? What messages were given to you when you were young that told you who you are? Can you remember when someone or some experience first handed you the baggage you've been carrying around? Take a moment to acknowledge that experience, the message, and release it.

That baggage is no longer serving you. It's keeping you down, pulling you away from your greatness.

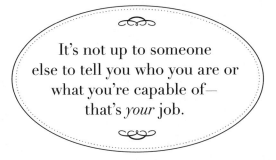

It's not up to someone else to tell you who you are or what you're capable of—that's *your* job.

Make sure you give yourself the right message.

I want you to dream big, without a single barrier getting in your imagination's way. If you see yourself helping millions, I want you to grasp that vision with all your might. Color that dream with details and pizazz. And when you feel you've pictured all the glitz your magical mind can muster, I want you to push yourself even further. Sell yourself on how Lady Boss living looks, without a single no stopping you or negative thought whipping you into a lack of belief.

19

BELIEVE IN YOUR VISION

I believe we've all been given fabulous, life-changing ideas and a unique song of our own. But we have to believe it. And we have to envision it. If you don't believe me, believe the deaf and blind activist and lecturer, Helen Keller.

"The only thing worse than being blind is having sight but no vision."

Without a vision, our soul withers, we dim our light, and we become cynical. The Bible says that where there's no vision, the people perish (Proverbs 29:18).

Research shows that the longer the members of an ancestry group have been in the US, the less likely they are to become millionaires, because they acclimate to a high-consumption lifestyle. On the other hand, first-generation Americans tend to be self-employed, and that increases their chance of becoming millionaires by 70 percent. What makes foreign-born US residents more likely to achieve their dreams? They see the opportunity and *seize* the day! I believe it's too easy for Americans to become complacent. We forget the incredible opportunity we have to dream larger-than-life victories for ourselves. Your life is a stunning masterpiece you can paint with your own brush. But you can't paint without a dream.

My great-grandmother Francine was born and raised in Germany. In 1925, she received a letter from her boyfriend asking her to start a life with him in America. She was nineteen at the time. She wrestled with that decision for a long time, weighing the risks and rewards. She decided to jump (not tiptoe) out on faith, put it all on the line, and board a ship to America. She left everything behind for the American dream.

How many of us would've become paralyzed with fear, imagining every awful danger? Imagine the barrage of questions she must've asked herself: *What if my beau isn't waiting for me when I arrive at Ellis Island? What if I don't like living in a totally new world? What if I don't succeed?*

I believe she abandoned fear because she refused to live an "ordinary" life. In that moment, she disciplined her mind to dominate her doubts (more on that in Key #2). She envisioned new experiences and focused on opportunities instead of dwelling on all the potential pitfalls. I've got to think she imagined America in all its splendor and what it had to offer her. I often picture myself as that young woman, German-born, naive to what life in the United States was like, sailing thousands of miles on a ship with little more than a letter and a prayer.

Francine was one ballsy lady. I have her to thank for my willingness to take risks! Once she arrived in the United States, she never returned to Germany. She drew a line in the sand. She gave herself the chance to succeed and to change the trajectory of her family legacy forever. Because she had tremendous faith and grit, she seized her vision.

Every person who has achieved massive success first dared to dream and then worked hard to make their vision a reality. Here's how I look at it: if you want to be the CEO of a company of your own design, it's a thousand times more likely to happen if you have a clear picture of what that looks like. How else will you drive yourself to get it done? Your dream company needs a CEO, and it might as well be you, right? Once you envision your ultimate Lady Boss life, devise a plan in baby steps and go after it.

21

Dream God-sized dreams.
If your dreams don't
scare you, your dreams
aren't big enough.

IT'S BIGGER THAN YOU

The beauty of your purpose is that it's a grand one, not only intended for your enjoyment. (Sorry, babe.) Lady Bosses are striving for greatness for the good of the whole. If your dreams only benefit you, it's time to check your priorities!

What's your grander purpose? Think about it: What ignites your passion and sets your soul on fire? What motivates you to dig deeper and drive harder than what seems rational to the average person?

Never allow average-minded people to make you feel guilty for playing all out. Cast a vision for what's possible—not just for you, but for your community and those future Lady Bosses with their eyes on you.

When you authentically play *all* out, magic happens.

22

If you connect with the core of your calling, you'll be unstoppable. In turn, your Lady Boss light will fire others up and empower them to reach beyond their imagination. The power and impact of pursuing your purpose is reflected beautifully in Marianne Williamson's remarkable book *A Return to Love: Reflections on the Principles from "A Course in Miracles"*, where she writes:

> *Our deepest fear is not that we are inadequate. Our deepest fear is that we are powerful beyond measure. It is our light, not our darkness that most frightens us. We ask ourselves, Who am I to be brilliant, gorgeous, talented, fabulous? Actually, who are you not to be? You are a child of God. Your playing small does not serve the world. There is nothing enlightened about shrinking so that other people won't feel insecure around you. We are all meant to shine, as*

children do. We were born to make manifest the glory of God that is within us. It's not just in some of us; it's in everyone. And as we let our own light shine, we unconsciously give other people permission to do the same. As we are liberated from our own fear, our presence automatically liberates others.

Lady Boss Life Hack:
Visualize It and Take Action

I kicked off my career in 2007 and shortly after flew to Georgia for the company's awards gala. While at the event, feeling inspired and with a glimmer in my eye, I leaned over to my friend—let's call him Jack—and with excitement declared, "Next year at this time, I'll return as a senior director."

*Keeping it real, I wasn't **actually** sure if I could achieve it, but I called it out anyway. Sometimes you have to declare your victory before it can manifest. With a doubtful smirk on his face, Jack said, "I'll believe it when I see it. Good luck, kid." I wanted to disappear. I felt two inches tall. I respected Jack, so his comment especially hurt. But suddenly, a sense of anger erupted inside me. I'll show him who's boss! I thought to myself.*

23

The biggest growth in my life often happens when I turn doubt and intimidation into an opportunity to kick butt. I want to show my doubters who's boss! Needless to say, at the following year's awards gala, with my senior director plaque in hand, I proudly winked at Jack as I took my seat . . . because that's what Lady Bosses do. #Winning.

SEE IT TO BELIEVE IT

Jim Carrey, the hilarious actor, said his father could've also been an exceptional comedian, but he didn't believe it was possible. His dad made the conservative choice and did the "safe" thing. He became an accountant. When Jim was twelve, his father was let go from that "safe" job, and his family struggled and did whatever they could to survive.

My absolute favorite quote from Jim:

"You can fail at what you don't want, so you might as well take a chance on doing what you love."

—Jim Carrey

Jim made the decision early on that he was destined for greatness, regardless of the fact that he and his family lived in their Volkswagen van on a relative's lawn for a season. Poverty encompassed his circumstances, yet he didn't let the "facts" dictate his destiny. He had so much faith in this greatness that, at the age of ten, he mailed his resume to *The Carol Burnett Show*. Talk about envisioning his ultimate dream life! Jim saw himself on the big screen from an early age. Then he took a step to bring his vision to light. Raise your hand if you were doing that at ten years old!

By 1990, Jim seemed to be going nowhere. The average person might have gone back to life by default, which in his case meant struggling to make it as a comic in L.A. But Jim did something else. He was certain he was going to the top— he had his vision. Though he was discouraged, he disciplined his disappointment, drove his beat-up Toyota to the top of a hill, and forced himself to visualize what was possible.

On that hill, Jim Carrey wrote himself a check for $10 million. He took it a step further and put in the notation line, "for acting services rendered." He dated it Thanksgiving 1995, and shoved it in his wallet. When 1995 came around five years later, Jim had starred in *Ace Ventura: Pet Detective*, *The Mask*, and *Liar, Liar*. His film fee had escalated to $20 million per film.

What are you doing today to propel yourself forward with passion toward your ultimate purpose and vision for your life? Are you letting your environment or the people around you dictate your destiny and define your future? You're in complete control of where you want to go in life. Your vision is possible, but you need a game plan with your destination in mind every step of the way.

"If you're going to answer the call and you're going to transform and you're going to change, get ready. It is not a day at the beach."

—Elizabeth Gilbert

Your background does not define you. Also, degrees do not define you! News flash: even if you dropped out of college or didn't go in the first place, that doesn't mean you have to settle for a low-paying, "trading hours for dollars" job the rest of your life. You could join the ranks of these Lady Bosses without college degrees: Oprah, Rachael Ray, Maya Angelou, Joyce Meyer, Adele, Anna Wintour, Mary Kay Ash, Ellen DeGeneres, and Coco Chanel, to name a few.

In almost every conversation, someone is buying and someone is selling. Are you buying the lies that you're not good enough or you don't have what it takes? Stop buying and start selling. Start selling yourself on how truly phenomenal you are, and go a step further to envision what *your* phenomenal is. Sell yourself on how incredible you are, and make a power move toward one of your God-sized dreams right now. Do it now. Sell yourself on the greatness inside you. Your beliefs will ultimately guide you to success or failure. It's completely your choice.

"The most courageous act is still to think for yourself. Aloud."

— Coco Chanel

The common denominator that almost all successful people possess is a passion and zeal for life. We all need a powerful vision for our lives—a vision so riveting and compelling it not only drives us to do whatever it takes to achieve it, but also gets others fired up about changing their lives, too. When you have buy-in from your tribe (more about this in Key #9), there is no cap on what you can accomplish.

26

LADY BOSS
BOLD MOVES

*(Use hashtag #UnleashYourLadyBoss
to keep us up to date on your Lady Boss wins!)*

1. Make the decision to become a Lady Boss and stick to it. Sign and date the Lady Boss Contract (visit unleashyourladyboss.com/powerplan).

2. Ask yourself, "What's my grander purpose?" What ignites your passion and sets your soul on fire? Go to a quiet place (Jim Carrey went to the top of a hill), perhaps lie on your yoga mat, and envision with intention where you are ten years from now. This is a no-limits zone, so dream big, sister. If your dreams don't scare you, they aren't big enough.

3. Write out five "I am" statements that shatter your current status quo. Writing in the present tense will help seal your vision as you shift your mindset on purpose. Go big and scoot the "what ifs" out of your way. (Examples: I am a business owner speaking at five national conferences annually. I am a steward of great wealth. I am highly favored and blessed to be a blessing. I am in love with the projects I have in process and the clients who are finding me.)

27

LADY BOSS
ACTION STEPS
AND AHA'S

DOMINATE YOUR DOUBTS

#BossYourBS

"It is in your moments of decision that your destiny is shaped."

—Tony Robbins

29

"**W**ho do you think you are?" demanded Tom (not his real name), my angry prospect sitting across the table from me at Starbucks. "Do you really think *you* are going to be successful? You're eighteen! You have no business experience *and* no credibility. If I were you, I'd get a real job and make something of my life. Good luck, kid!"

I didn't realize it at that time, but this encounter would change my life. *Screw him!* I thought to myself as I tried to shake off his critical comments. But it didn't take long for doubts to seep in.

Maybe he's right. What the heck am I doing? Who am I kidding? It's over. Entrepreneurship isn't for me! It's too hard! It's not worth it! I have been at this day after day, working hard, and it seems like I am going nowhere.

I was devastated. Not to mention, here was another prospect telling me no, which seemed at the time to be the unfortunate norm. But that encounter wasn't only about his rejecting me. Those comments cut far deeper than the normal no. This guy shouted doubt, unbelief, and fear right into my core. What the heck was I doing trying to make my vision a reality?

Never in the history of the company I partnered with had anyone hit the goal I was shooting for as a teenager. Maybe he was right. Maybe I should get a "real job" instead of pursuing my dream. Even though I knew I was meant for more, I started to believe that the lack of traction I was making was a sign. It was time to call Mama P.

My mom, known as "Mama P." by the many college students she's mentored over the years, has been my biggest cheerleader and best friend since the day I was born. She is the kindest, most giving, and selfless servant-leader I've ever known. I may be a bit biased, but even many of my friends refer to her as "the white Oprah"!

I'm pretty sure that if you set foot in her house on Christmas Day unannounced, within five minutes she would pull out presents from her gift closet and give you some of the best gifts you've ever been given. Mama P. is phenomenal. And I needed her insight and inspiration desperately. Whenever I feel the world falling apart around me, she invites me to walk around the "therapy pond" near my childhood home, and together we solve the world's problems. After one round of walking (about one and a half miles) and talking out the "difficulty," I often feel the weight of the world lift from my shoulders. Mama P., on the other hand, leaves quite exhausted from pouring belief and encouragement into this little blonde emotional basket case!

After my meeting with Tom, I picked up the phone, crying hysterically, and invited myself to Mama P.'s so she could help cure my devastation. I was banking on our usual "blessed resolution" to resurface as it always had. This particular evening was different. My mind raced as I drove to her house. Again, doubts attacked my every thought. *What if my dreams really aren't possible? What if I keep working for years and years and I fail and fail and fail? What are all my friends going to think? Why does life have to be so damn hard?*

When I arrived at Mama P.'s door, I was a hot mess, my face smeared in mascara. I looked like a pumpkin with the candle gone out. On our first lap around the pond, she gave me the usual pep talk. Holding my hand, she said in her loving way, "You can do this. You are my champion. You've got everything it takes!"

She was saying all the things that would normally pull me out of my funk, but not this time. I wasn't having it. Self-doubt had worked a number on me like never before. Tom's words had truly cut that deep. So she suggested walking around the pond a second time to work her "magic." I agreed reluctantly, but even after the second round, her words still felt empty. I felt wrecked and defeated, and I didn't want to hear the "you've got what it takes" speech.

As we approached the house, I let out another burst of tears. My mom began to lose her patience. Her ever-present, sweet demeanor seemed to evaporate in an instant. Mama P. took a deep breath and braced herself—she knows I'm a firecracker. She also knew I probably wasn't going to take her next statement well, but it had to be said.

"Stefanie, if you can't stand the heat, get out of the kitchen. Entrepreneurship is not for everyone, and it certainly sounds like it's not for you!"

I was shocked. I was flooded with a barrage of emotions. *What? Are you kidding me? My own mother doesn't even believe in me. What the heck? Who does she think she is? Who*

31

gave her the right to tell me what I can and cannot do? I could feel the rage rising on the inside.

"Screw this. I'm done. This isn't worth it!" I screamed. I couldn't believe my own mother was against me.

I turned to her, and with all the hurt I could muster, yelled, "Thanks for all the encouragement. I thought you loved me!"

How's that for drama? By now, I was running up the driveway. Then I slammed the front door in her face and ran downstairs into the bathroom and bawled for what seemed like forever. Tons of emotions flooded over me, and I began to question everything. I was suffering from a major case of PLOM (Poor Little Old Me) disease! I remember even yelling into the mirror, "God, why are you putting me through this? I'm in a terrible place!"

At that moment, I felt a strong presence come over me, followed by an unexplained moment of clarity. I heard an audible voice, plain as day, say,

Stefanie, I created you to live life by My design. I gave you a specific mission and calling. I put you on Earth to change people's lives. Are you willing to answer My call? The road ahead is going to be hard at times. But if it were easy, you wouldn't grow in your compassion or relate to the people you're meant to inspire. I'm creating a much stronger story within you. You'll have a life-changing testimony because of what you're going through. Your journey will be significant, and you'll fulfill a major part of your mission. Don't give up. You'll make a monumental impact and influence the masses if you don't abandon your dream. If you fight through this, I'll use you in mighty ways. But the choice is yours.

I was speechless. To this day, I still get chills when I think about hearing God's voice so clearly. I think God speaks to us more than we realize. But we have to be in the right mindset to hear Him.

After hearing His voice, my emotions calmed almost immediately, and I had a strong inner peace I'd never experienced before. I looked myself in the mirror and with conviction declared, "I don't care how long it takes to become one of the top leaders in my company. I will get there, and I will change countless lives in the process. I will get out of my own way and show others they can reach the American dream if they're willing to run for it. I will be a beacon of light *and* a trailblazer of hope. I will inspire others to their greatness! With God's help, I'm going to write the history books!" How's that for kicking doubt, fear, and anxiety in the butt?

I dried my tears, changed my attitude, thanked my mom, gave her a big hug, and set out on my mission to change lives. More people said no to me than I prefer to recall, but one year later, I became the youngest female senior director in the billion-dollar international company that I partnered with. I don't share my story to brag. I share my story to challenge you to step out in faith and to dare you to do the "impossible" and write the history books. In the movie *The Pursuit of Happyness*, Chris Gardner, played by Will Smith, said it best when he gave this advice to his son:

33

"Don't ever let someone tell you, you can't do something. Not even me. You got a dream, you gotta protect it. When people can't do something themselves, they want to tell you you can't do it. You want something, go get it. Period."

After hearing God's voice, I made the decision to never turn back. It's interesting that in life, once you make the absolute decision that you're going to go forward, no matter what, in spite of all obstacles, things begin falling into place. Once I made the *decision,* my business kicked into high gear. I wasn't riding the emotional roller coaster of self-doubt anymore. I began to dominate my doubts! Once the internal questions quieted, I could finally make progress. My vision was crystal clear. I set my sights on shattering the glass ceiling in my company. I would show them that even a young, blonde female could be a rock star. It wasn't a matter of *if* anymore, but a matter of *when.*

HUSH YOUR HATERS, DAZZLE YOUR DOUBTERS

I wonder how many of our problems we'd solve if we didn't assume they were unsolvable. How many higher levels would we reach if we thought we could accomplish the "impossible"? Part of the problem is that we're listening to the wrong "experts" in our lives—like Tom.

Who are you allowing to tell you that you can't, shouldn't, or won't be the Lady Boss you're destined to be? Is it a sibling? Is it your boyfriend or husband? Is it your parents? A teacher from grade school? Often we allow others to define who we are and what we're capable of.

Don't let the peanut gallery run your life.

Even when they mean well, you know more about the fire burning within you than anyone else. Sometimes, others' fear creates fears in us we didn't have in the first place. I believe one of the top reasons people fail or give up is that they listened to their friends, family, and neighbors. But try paying your bills with the opinions of the haters and doubters. Good luck!

Respect your doubters, but do in your heart what God is calling you to do, regardless of how others in your life take it! It's not an easy task to put their fears on the back burner. But it's far worse to have your head hit the pillow knowing you're making everyone else around you happy while your own soul is withering. This is what happens when you're not living *your* true calling and following *your* destiny. Your future is more important than the opinions of others. Run *your* race!

Remember that the voice inside you will continue to gnaw at you until you answer the call. Your God-given idea, story, and business venture that will set the world on fire will continue to resurface—you can't escape it. Don't let the song inside you go unsung. Once you've envisioned what your ideal future looks like, decide to make it a reality by shifting your mindset into "get after it" mode and keeping your eyes on the prize.

35

> *"It is never too late to be who you might have been."*
> —Anonymous

Lady Boss, it's not a matter of *if* you can do it, whatever your *it* is. It's only a matter of how and how fast. I decided to force myself to figure it out, and that shift in mindset made the journey more enjoyable. I stopped listening to the negative voices designed to throw me off course.

Sister, you will have doubts. But if you have the right ammo in your back pocket, you can dominate any doubts that come your way. You might need a ready-to-go scripture or pep talk. Whatever ammo works for you, always be prepared with a verbal tiara you can put on to get your sassy back. Here's one I use: "Your mind is powerful. This obstacle is not meant to defeat you but to drive you to your divine destiny. You are smart. You will figure it out. You've got this."

You have to hype yourself up when the going gets tough, because emotional indecision is lethal. It will exhaust you if you let it. Before Mama P.'s "if you can't stand the heat, get out of the kitchen" moment, I was your typical drama queen. I followed my feelings like a girl on the hunt for a date on Friday night. If my feelings, especially my doubts, told me to go left, I did.

I learned an important lesson in the bathroom with God that day:

*Life is won and lost
in the mind.*

When you feel as if you've got all the confidence in the world, your mind will play tricks on you the next day. Ladies, the entrepreneurial roller coaster is real. In the morning you're getting a no. By afternoon you'll have a win. Then you'll overanalyze your win and question yourself, and by the end of the day you're exhausted. Riding this mental roller coaster day in and day out takes a toll. As Lady Bosses, we have to strengthen our mental muscles daily. We need to command our mind to focus on our vision, regardless of our feelings. We can't believe the lies our minds tell us when we're running on empty.

YOU GOT THE GOODS

One of my good friends—I'll call her Ashley—contacted me to help get her business off the ground. As we went through her strategy session and set goals, I challenged her to make five prospecting calls to challenge her comfort zone and make something happen. Ashley wasn't thrilled, but after a few pushes, she begrudgingly agreed. I asked for the name of the first person on her list. She said it was her mother. I gave her the exact script of what to say and had her practice on me first. The practice run went stellar.

"Okay," I said. "Let's go. Give your mom a call."

Ashley's eyes immediately got big, and with terror in her voice she warned, "You don't know my mom. I shouldn't call her."

I was dumbfounded. "You hired me as your coach, and I want to see you succeed. Get on the phone! You want to rock this, right?"

With trepidation in her eyes, Ashley picked up the phone and dialed her mom's number. Within the first minutes of the phone call, I could hear a negative voice filled with disdain on the other end. The intoxicating energy suffocated the entire room. Then I heard, "What on earth are you doing? Why do you want to do anything more than your full-time job? You're foolish, and you have three kids to care for."

It went downhill from there until I whispered in Ashley's other ear, "Get off the phone!"

You could see the fight for her dream wither against her mother's defeating disappointment. Tears started to stream down Ashley's face. I was heated. Her own mother was stealing her dream! What mother does that? I'm blessed enough to have a mom who would buy hot dogs from me if she were vegan. Unfortunately, in my years of coaching Lady

Bosses, I've found that pushback from our own inner circles is more prevalent and deadly than I would've ever dreamed.

I hugged Ashley and encouraged her, "Girl, don't you let *anyone*, even your own mother, steal your dream. This road will not be easy, but if you make the decision that you won't let anything or anyone take this from you, you will succeed. This is your life and your choice." I told her we could be done for the day and that I would come back tomorrow. We'd need to hit it from a whole new angle. She didn't seem convinced, but she agreed.

As I left, I prayed that she would be strengthened and not let outside forces rip anything from her. The following day, she looked down and dejected.

"You've got the goods!" I reminded her as we set out on our game plan. "Don't you dare let anyone tell you otherwise. You have everything within you that you need to accomplish your dream. This is just the start of your stilettos hitting the first of many bumps on the boulevard. You've got to learn to dominate your doubts. It's now up to you to choose the life you want and choose your hard."

I'll explain it to you the way I explained to Ashley. There are two types of hard: First, getting out of your comfort zone is hard. But, ladies, staying broke is hard, too. So, you've got to choose your hard. In my years as a coach, I've found that every woman says she wants to be successful, but most don't want to do the hard work it takes to get there.

Living life by design is hard; living life by default is hard. Choose your hard.

I could see a Lady Boss rise up from inside Ashley as she confidently declared, "I am meant for more, and I choose a life by design. Let's do this!" My heart exploded with joy. I was lit up with her, and we readied ourselves to dig right in. From there, she powered through her calls. She was kicking butt and taking names, and I couldn't have been prouder. Even though she had a full-time job, she was willing to make the short-term sacrifice for the long-term gain. That's how we Lady Bosses roll. We set our game plan and make it happen.

As we approached the end of the month, Ashley only needed to secure one more account to reach her goal. She was nervous, but I coached her to call someone on her "chicken list." She did. It was the last day of the month, and we hustled to our local java joint (coffee makes everything easier). We went through the overview with Ashley's prospect, a delightful woman we'll call Sarah. As we ended, Sarah started tearing up. *Oh boy,* I thought. *Here we go again. How is Ashley going to take this?*

As Ashley wrapped the meeting, Sarah said, "Ashley, you have no idea what a godsend it is that you called me. I've been praying that someone would come into my life and help me. I've been at my wit's end. I'm so grateful. I feel like it's been forever since I've felt any hope, and I believe this is the answer! You're amazing. I'm so blessed by you!"

I started crying, Ashley started crying, and it felt like a full-on Kumbaya session broke out right in the middle of the coffee shop. Everyone around us probably thought we were nuts, but I couldn't have cared less. I looked intently at Ashley and said, "Sister, you should be so proud! You didn't let your mother dim your light. You're going to be such an inspiration to countless women. How incredible does it feel that you're the light in someone else's life? This wouldn't have happened if you hadn't dominated your doubts and had a

39

burning desire to run after your purpose and change lives in the process."

I get jazzed when I watch women create a vision for themselves, put together a game plan, and own their dream. I don't believe it's a reality in this economy to "land your dream job" anymore. The corporate "climb the ladder" to a secure job approach isn't so secure. Research shows that the average employee changes professions seven different times before she retires. You have to create your dream life. You have to show up and own your vision day in and day out, even when you don't feel like it. And when doubt creeps in, which it always will, decide to dominate it.

40

LADY BOSS
BOLD MOVES

*(Use hashtag #UnleashYourLadyBoss
to keep us up to date on your Lady Boss wins!)*

1. Design your Lady Boss arsenal. Create a disciplined regimen of intentional actions, mantras, and sacrifices you can make right away to demolish the barriers in your way. (Examples: give up television shows that don't uplift you and replace them with inspirational podcasts that do, or write down an encouraging statement to recite when things get tough.)

2. Read *Fearless & Fabulous* by Cara Alwill Leyba. This book is a must-read for Lady Bosses who want to kick fear in the ass.

3. Don't sweat every doubt that rears its ugly head, and don't take it personally when a doubter tries to steer you from your path. Go to www.unleashyourladyboss.com/powerplan to access the "Dominate Your Doubt Affirmations" worksheet. Write your affirmations down and post them somewhere visible.

41

LADY BOSS
ACTION STEPS
AND AHA'S

DARE TO JUMP

#ReadyAimFire

"I never thought I'd be successful. It seems in my own mind that in everything I've undertaken I've never quite made the mark. But I've always been able to put disappointments aside. Success isn't about the end result; it's about what you learn along the way."

—Vera Wang

Stepping into your purpose requires looking over the cliff, knowing you can't predict the outcome, kicking off those stilettos, and jumping anyway. It's completely terrifying but completely worth the high!

Aren't you jazzed to be the designated driver of your life? I've spoken to many women who don't realize the opportunities that lie inside them. They're not living their dreams because they don't know how. Or their fear has them stuck in limbo—knowing their purpose but fearful of the fallout postleap. One of the biggest Lady Boss killers is paralysis by analysis. So many women don't think they can make a move

43

until they know *exactly* how things will play out. Sorry, girlfriend. You'll never know exactly how anything will play out as you grow your empire. But you have to trust your intuition and that the Big Guy upstairs has your back.

Lady Boss Killer:
Perfectionism . . . Solution:
Stop Analyzing and Start *Acting*
#BreakOutOfPerfectionPrison

As we've discussed, the women who make their dreams a reality start by believing in themselves. Then they step out in faith and make their dreams happen. That's it. They jump, trusting the net will appear. Your doubts will tell you jumping is dangerous—or worse, that there is no net. Thank God you'll have your Lady Boss Arsenal to dominate those obnoxious doubts!

Another barrier to making dreams reality is that so many of us see ourselves as caretakers. We take care of everyone's needs around us but neglect to take care of ourselves. Our culture enforces this mindset, so it's important that we don't forget to nurture our own well-being. It's okay to say no sometimes! It means giving yourself time to focus on what you really want. And yes, sometimes it means splurging for that massage or fancy purse—whatever it takes to refill your tank!

When I was writing this book, I really had no idea what it looked like to write and publish a book. Was I a little freaked out? Of course. Did I have my doubts? Absolutely. Did I question my ability? Heck yeah! But I felt a relentless pull from inside that told me becoming an author was part of my purpose. I'd contemplated writing a book for years, but the what-ifs always got in my way. When it was finally time—and I knew it was time, deep in my soul—I had to *choose* the dream. I got sick of just thinking about it and pulled out my Lady Boss ammo. Not only did I have to choose to believe in myself, that I *could* do it, but I had to prioritize my dream. I had to focus and say no, sometimes to people I love who wanted my attention and energy. A Lady Boss has to choose the confidence *and* the focus at the same time.

There will never be a perfect time to make your move. You have to *create* the perfect time.

Sister, it's time for you to play a bigger game and help more people on a massive scale. The day I decided I was going to start writing and not turn back was the day I changed the trajectory of my life and many others. That's the power of a bigger-game decision. Once you make it, doors will open, lives will change, you'll dominate your doubts, and you'll leave them in the dust. But sometimes you'll have to feel the fear and jump first.

I believe the law of attraction starts working on overdrive when you jump off the cliff and make a bigger-game decision. I was amazed that once I decided to write a book, people "randomly" appeared from nowhere. "Divine connections," as I call them, came to me and asked how they could take part in the vision! When you set goals, trust me when I say that all of heaven will move to help you fulfill them—as long as *you* are moving too. I've written down goals that my doubts and fears told me I could never accomplish. By average standards, these goals were totally out of the realm of possibility. But average standards are not Lady Bosses' standards. We make the impossible possible.

Once you make the decision to make a goal happen no matter what, the "how" will take care of itself. Here's my bottom-line perspective: If I step out in faith and fail, then . . . oh well. I don't lose sleep over it and neither should you. What I fear more than failure is lying on my deathbed regretting the chances I didn't take, wondering about what-ifs and how I could've changed the world. I'd much rather live with "oh wells." And the rush is so much better than wishing you would've taken a chance.

Remember this: a bigger-game decision is the difference between living an ordinary life and an extraordinary life!

TAKE MORE RISKS

In a recent survey, elderly people were asked what their biggest regret in life was. Many responded, "I wish I had taken more risks."

At the end of your life, looking back, you don't want to live with regrets. Take that risk.

My dad tells the story of attending a men's retreat for our church. He was a young evangelist at a serious crossroads in his life, where his ministry was phasing out. He was seeking divine guidance on his next step. A man across the aisle at the chapel service came up to him and said, "I think God wants to tell you something today. It's pretty simple; I think he wants you to take more risks!"

Dad never forgot those three words: *take more risks!* He began to look for bigger opportunities, to be open to things that maybe he would've turned down before but where he would be able to play a bigger game.

Shortly after that, in 1991, an opportunity to become an independent marketing representative at a startup company came along. Before then, my dad would've definitely turned it down. But after discussing it, both he and my mom decided to go for it. They found out they were pretty good at it. Soon, their business was soaring. They kept at it through the tough times. Long story short, they have each become one of the top ten producers of all time for their company.

47

Lady Boss Life Hack:

Once you accomplish the "impossible," it gives the masses permission to do the same.

As many of you know, I'm a runner, so I'm particularly inspired by this next story. Experts said for years that it was impossible for the human body to run a four-minute mile. Then along came Roger Bannister, the man who shattered what the "authorities" said was out of the realm of human possibility. On May 6, 1954, in Oxford, England, Roger Bannister broke the four-minute mile, running the distance in 3:59.4. How did he do it? He relentlessly visualized breaking the barrier in his mind before even setting foot on the track. He decided he would accomplish the impossible and convinced his body to do what it needed to do to achieve the task at hand.

His teammates paced him and pushed his limits, while his coach drilled the belief into him even when he didn't believe in himself. (More on this in Key #9, where we talk about building your tribe.) Now, more than four hundred American runners have broken the four-minute-mile barrier. In fact, it has been lowered by seventeen seconds. Once you break into new territory, you'll inspire others to realize their possibilities and follow in your footsteps.

As I've coached many women through the years, I often hear, "Well, I want to go forward, but I'm not quite sure how to get there. Where do I even begin?" My answer: begin right where you are. You may or may not be aware of this, but let me put this out there: Sometimes leaders don't know exactly how they'll get there, but they keep it movin', one step at a time. The biggest lie you can tell yourself is that playing a bigger game is too hard. The other lie is that it's not the right time. I'll say it again: jump and the net will appear. Get out there and break records. Show the "experts" what's up!

"No one else knows what they are doing either!"

—Ricky Gervais

Another fear that might be keeping you from leaping into your destiny is the false belief that you're too old or too young. I've been blessed to know and admire Lady Bosses who are eighteen and Lady Bosses in their eighties. One of the world's premier women's designers, Vera Wang, didn't enter the fashion industry until she was forty. Laura Ingalls Wilder was sixty-five when she published her first book, which kicked off the beloved *Little House on the Prairie* series and turned into twelve books and a monumentally successful television show that lasted ten years and is still in syndication today. Renowned American folk artist Grandma Moses started her astonishing painting career at seventy-eight. In 2006, one of her paintings sold for $1.2 million.

Imagine the fear that could've prevented these legends from shattering glass ceilings. I'm sure they were told they were too old, out of their league, or trying to play a game that was too big. Thank goodness they didn't listen to their doubters and haters!

Lady Boss Life Hack:

Choose to be bummed for a minute, not a month . . .
save your energy for what truly matters!

SHOW THE GOOD
OL' BOYS WHO'S BOSS

When I was eighteen, I was excited to kick off my own business. Naturally, I wanted to share my news with a few of my closest friends. I called a friend whom I really looked up to and admired—let's call him Brad. After telling him my good news, Brad cleared his throat and said, "Stef, until you make more than one thousand dollars a month, don't call me again." *Well, that was sweet,* I thought as I hung up the phone. But, you better believe that motivated this little firecracker to make it happen that month!

Not long after, I called another close guy friend I thought was pretty legit in the business world. I took him to dinner and shared my business model and overview with him. He looked me straight in the eye and made quite a snide remark. Later, I got wind of how he was also saying demeaning things about me to our core circle of friends.

Did it initially hurt? Yes, no doubt! I could've let that deflate me, and for two hot seconds it did. But, my *why* was bigger than that dude's ego—and let me tell you, that makes for a huge *why*. Busting through others' BS takes practice, but if you can be bummed for a minute instead of a month, you'll make so much more progress, *and* you'll save your energy for the important things.

Side note: Brad called me two years after our phone call and said, "I hear you're killing it in that business I wasn't too high on."

"Yep," I said. "I feel very blessed, and it's been quite the ride, Brad."

After a few moments of awkward silence, he said, "I'd like to sit down to make sure I'm not interested." Not too long after that, we sat down at a Starbucks, teamed up in business, and the rest is history.

One of my favorite Bible verses is 1 Timothy 4:12, which says, "Don't let anyone think less of you because you are young. Be an example to all believers in what you say, in the way you live, in your love, your faith, and your purity."

Lady Boss, be the example and shine your light. I'm blown away by the number of friends who've said—since they heard I cofounded Lady Boss Empire, wrote a book, bought a vacation home in Florida, and hit senior director in my late teens and executive director by twenty-two—that they are going to run after their dreams, too. When you dare to jump, it's amazing how it ignites the greatness in those around you. It's such a rewarding feeling.

What "impossible" venture do you want to accomplish? What are the "four-minute miles" in your life that are holding you back personally and professionally? Who are the "Brads" you need to release to keep moving? What are you willing to sacrifice to make it happen? When I decided I was going to go for the gold and break records, I "burned my ships." I decided for the next twelve months I would make crazy sacrifices to make my dream a reality. I would show others in my space what was possible for them.

When I decided I wasn't going to turn back and instead built my dream business, it was unreal how momentum started to build almost immediately. Things sped up and I was all in. Week after week, I worked day and night. Folks thought I was crazy. On the outside, people asked why I put in so many hours. "Why the hustle?" they asked. This is the best way I've heard it said:

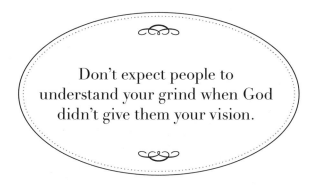

Don't expect people to understand your grind when God didn't give them your vision.

51

Boom.

Lady Boss, I challenge you to dig deeper, drive harder, and challenge your thoughts about what's possible. This is what daring to jump is all about. My guess is that you'll be blown away by the doors that will open for you and the moves you'll be able to make.

LADY BOSS
BOLD MOVES

*(Use hashtag #UnleashYourLadyBoss
to keep us up to date on your Lady Boss wins!)*

❧ ——————— ❧

1. Activate your "Bigger Game" Board of Advisors. Select a key group of mentors who inspire you and have dared to jump. Make sure your board is filled with risk takers, boundless visionaries, and bosses. Interact with your board monthly.

2. What's one power move you could make to break out of whatever is holding you back? Take that leap and get 'er done! What's a reasonable deadline to set for yourself?

3. Distance yourself from doubters, haters, and the fearful. You can't reach the next level with negative energy pulling you backwards. Make a list of the Lady Boss killers in your life (people, habits, lifestyle choices, and beliefs) and scratch one off your list every week until it's completely empty.

LADY BOSS
ACTION STEPS
AND AHA'S

_____

_____

_____

_____

_____

_____

_____

_____

_____

_____

_____

_____

_____

_____

_____

53

BECOME A GOAL DIGGER

#DreamWithADeadline

"A goal without a game plan is like a girl without glitz. It works, but let's get real . . . something is missing. Combine them and magic happens!"

—Stefanie Peters

How often have you set a goal—to lose a few pounds, to send more thank-you notes, to land a huge client—and under mounting pressure, you weren't able to get 'er done? How many times have you woken to discover the next year is rolling around and you never read that book on your nightstand, got that passport, completed that business plan, wrote that first chapter for your book . . . the list goes on. I want to let you in on a little Lady Boss secret: many people complicate goals.

Goals are simply dreams
with a deadline.

And guess what? The major ingredient to living an epic life is *focus*.

When we set a goal and don't reach it, it's often for one of three reasons. 1) We don't hold ourselves accountable; 2) we set a wrong goal for the wrong reason; or 3) we set a right goal, but we're *waiting* for the "right time" before we go after it. Here are the three secrets to becoming a goal crusher:

1. Set reachable goals that align with your vision.
2. Create a killer game plan and set realistic deadlines.
3. Fiercely focus like your life depends on it!

In reality, your life does depend on it! The quickest way to lose momentum is to let a God-given goal fall by the wayside.

STEP 1: START WITH YOUR WHY AND CHOOSE YOUR WORD

Do you have a goal for this year? At the beginning of my career, I was so laser-focused on my goals that I would sometimes forget to enjoy the journey and the reason *why* I was running after them. One of the best tools I've found for avoiding this dangerous trap is choosing one word for the year.

By choosing just one word to focus on, you position yourself for not only a successful year but a significant year. I'm obsessed with this! This simple practice helps you keep per-

55

spective. You'll be able to clearly target who you want to become and how you want to impact people on the way toward your goals. I believe the person you become on the way to the goal is far more important than the goal itself. Ultimately, goals are there to help you become the rock star God created you to be. Sister, the marvelous rewards and accomplishments you achieve along the way are icing on the cake.

I highly recommend reading, *One Word That Will Change Your Life* by Dan Britton, Jimmy Page, and Jon Gordon. And while designing your goals list, check out *Design Your Best Year Ever* by Darren Hardy, the former publisher of *Success* magazine. These books will change your life like they did mine! And while you're at it, subscribe to *Success* magazine.

After I designate my one word for the year (my word this year is *impact*), I set "hallelujah" goals, which are my over-the-top goals. Next, I set my "it's all good" goals, which are my baseline goals. When you set goals, push your limits and challenge yourself, but also give yourself enough breathing room. If life doesn't go exactly as planned (which it won't, in case you were wondering) you have a fallback position with an "it's all good" goal. Give the "hallelujah" goals your best shot, and let the chips fall where they may.

STEP 2: PLAN, DO, REVIEW

In this stage, I take my vision (dial back to Key #1 for a recap) and break it into bite-sized, long-term goals of what I can do this year, month, week, and today. I set these long-term goals in eight different life areas: business, financial, physical, mental, family, spiritual, lifestyle, and relationships. Then, under each of those eight, I write my top three goals. I narrow down those goals to the top one in each area. I then take it a step further and assign each one a deadline. Each week, I star my top three goals for the week, game-plan them out, and then fiercely focus on what I need to do daily to make them happen. Below is an example of how to lay out your goals.

BUSINESS

(Examples: start a business, acquire a new skill, start a blog, write a book, take a social media course, delegate tasks, improve time management skills, grow to be number one in your industry, create a YouTube channel for your business, or build a creative team.)

1.

2.

3.

FINANCIAL

(Examples: get out of debt, pay off student loans, save for retirement, cut up credit cards, take a financial class, automate bill payment, buy a home, pay off a car loan, become financially independent, create multiple streams of residual income, or donate regularly.)

1.

2.

3.

57

PHYSICAL

(Examples: lose fifteen pounds, eat healthier, work out daily, drink more water, schedule annual doctor appointments, start seeing a chiropractor, get a monthly massage, improve wardrobe, see a fashion consultant, improve physical appearance, see a hairstylist, take a new workout class, reduce sugar intake, or see a nutritionist.)

1.

2.

3.

MENTAL

(Examples: read personal development books, take a course to expand your mind, get organized, make time for self-care, choose to be less stressed, choose to enjoy life, or choose to be happy and content while challenging your limits.)

1.

2.

3.

FAMILY

(Examples: create family fun days, find Mr./Ms. Right, send birthday card/encouragement card to close family/friends, plan a weekly date night, save for a dream vacation, or become a better mother/daughter/friend/girlfriend/wife.)

1.

2.

3.

SPIRITUAL

(Examples: get involved in a group within church, do daily devotionals, volunteer, take a mission trip, donate to a non-profit, pray/meditate daily, or create a foundation to fund a cause.)

1.

2.

3.

LIFESTYLE

(Examples: take a cruise to the Greek Isles, take up a new hobby, start salsa lessons, redo your home office, travel to and speak at a leadership conference, attend a tech conference, host a book signing, meet a VIP, or visit Facebook headquarters.)

1.

2.

3.

59

RELATIONSHIPS

(Examples: get a mentor, be a mentor, spend more time with friends, or cultivate and nurture relationships with like-minded achievers.)

1.

2.

3.

I'd love to be able to tell you that I accomplish every goal every time I write them down, but obviously you know this isn't true. That's where the Plan, Do, Review comes in. Every Sunday night, I reflect on the past week and evaluate what went well and what needs to be corrected, and I adjust priorities accordingly. I set up my week to rock it out again, and I try to avoid the pitfalls from the week before. This ensures I won't repeat the same mistakes and expect different results. That's the definition of insanity, right? When we activate this level of focus, our goals become SMART (specific, measurable, attainable, realistic, and timely, according to Peter F. Drucker's 1954 book, *The Practice of Management*).

Ladies, keep this in mind: slow progress is way better than no progress, but consistency is key in goal-setting. That's why it's so important to break the big goals into a game plan you can bite into daily.

I dreamed of creating multiple streams of residual income as a young entrepreneur. I knew my first step would be to buy an investment property. So I posted that goal on my dream board: to own my first investment property by age nineteen. I was intrigued with the potential of renters sending me a check every month, and I wanted to establish a lifelong stream of passive income.

I saved my hard-earned money and bought a foreclosure in 2008, purchasing it at the bottom of the housing bubble during the big recession. This townhouse would've gone for $225,000 a year or so prior, but I bought it for $105,000. Friends warned me that I might be buying too early and that housing prices might continue to fall. I said, "That's okay. If prices fall more, I'll just buy more properties!"

I purchased that brand-new, four-bedroom, three-bath, 1,770-square-foot townhouse in a beautiful neighborhood. Several years later, I paid it off and burned the mortgage in front of ten thousand cheering fans at my company convention. The company I partnered with gives awards for three levels of financial freedom: 1) paying off all your credit cards; 2) paying off all your debt except your mortgage, including all car loans; 3) becoming completely debt-free and having the exhilarating experience of burning your mortgage onstage. I love the fact that this company is rewarding people for becoming debt-free!

I now own a townhome free and clear. Wow! To be in my early twenties and own a gorgeous investment property debt-free was a dream come true. And you can reach your dreams too! But you have to dream the dream, set the goal, and then take massive action. Through that property alone, I've collected over $115,000 in rent, which is more than I paid for the property. If I keep that home for another fifty years, until I'm seventy-seven, I will have earned a total of $1.1 million. And that's if I never raise the rent; but rental prices in my area are going up every year, so I'll probably collect over $2 million, which is almost twice as much as the average American earns in their lifetime! Now that's working smart—and getting your money to work for you.

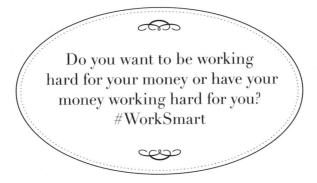

Do you want to be working
hard for your money or have your
money working hard for you?
#WorkSmart

The reason I shared that is so you know the power of dreaming big and working toward a goal every day, coupled with the power of investing for residual income. The combination is life changing.

I've since purchased three more properties and intend to keep on buying. I love real estate. I'd like to talk more about that, but I'll save it for my next book. Stay tuned!

BIG GOALS LEAD TO BIG LIVES

I recently saw a picture from the 1960s of a little black girl standing in front of the White House in Washington, DC. She had pestered her parents for months to take her there. At the time, she looked up at her parents and said, "I'll work in that house someday."

A black girlfriend of hers had recently been killed in a church bombing, and she had no reason to believe she'd ever work at the White House. She was a little black girl growing up in Birmingham, Alabama, and the chips were stacked against her. But her circumstances didn't keep her from dreaming and setting a goal. She had a destiny to fulfill, and she wasn't going to let her goal die.

Years later, she strode confidently into that same White House, shook the hand of President George W. Bush, and became one of the most powerful women in the world. Her name? Condoleezza Rice. She became Bush's national security advisor in 2001, and in 2005, Rice was promoted to secretary of state, becoming fourth in line to the presidency. That's the power of pursuing a goal and setting an intention.

I love watching the Olympics, especially seeing people reach goals they've worked toward for thousands of hours. When these athletes are interviewed and we hear their stories, I'm always overwhelmed by the amount of time and effort they've poured into reaching their goals.

Sixteen-year-old Sarah Hughes wasn't supposed to go to the 2002 Winter Olympics in Salt Lake City. At the Olympics, Sarah placed fourth in the short program, which seemingly put her out of contention for the gold medal. Just before she was about to skate in the long program, NBC's coverage cut to a video Sarah's mother had taken of little Sarah when she was five years old. Sarah's mom asked her, "What do you want to do when you grow up?" Little Sarah answered on video, "I want to go to the Olympics and win a gold medal!"

Sarah didn't just say she wanted to go to the Olympics; she emphatically declared that she wanted to win a gold medal. Sarah was crystal clear about her goal. NBC commentators said that Sarah looked extremely confident and relaxed. And Sarah didn't disappoint. She skated the program of her life, shocking her critics who said she wasn't in the running for a gold medal against legendary figure-skating champion Michelle Kwan.

Sarah Hughes won her gold medal! But actually, she had won it eleven years before, as a five-year-old girl setting a gigantic goal. When her picture hit the front cover of *Time* magazine, the official website of the Olympic Games called it "one of figure skating's greatest upsets."

Lady Bosses, Condoleezza Rice and Sarah Hughes aren't more special than you. Did they have some built-in advantage? No! In fact, the opposite is probably true; they both had built-in disadvantages. If they can achieve their goals, so can you. Cut the excuses and get after your goals! Simple. You've got greatness within you. And it's *your* job to bring it out.

63

LADY BOSS
BOLD MOVES

*(Use hashtag #UnleashYourLadyBoss
to keep us up to date on your Lady Boss wins!)*

1. Connect with the "why" behind your vision. This is the key to goal-setting. For inspiration, watch Simon Sinek's "Start with Why" TED Talk on YouTube. Once you know your "why," place reminders all around you.

2. Fill out the Lady Boss goal planner with your ten-year, five-year, one-year, and weekly game plans. To access a PDF, visit www.unleashyourladyboss.com/powerplan.

3. Share your goal sheet with a close friend and ask them to keep you accountable! I challenge you to share one banner goal publicly.

LADY BOSS
ACTION STEPS
AND AHA'S

_____

_____

_____

_____

_____

_____

_____

_____

_____

_____

_____

_____

_____

_____

65

CHISEL THE GOAL IN GRANITE

#InkIt

"Write the vision; inscribe it on tablets,
so he may run who reads it."
—Habakkuk 2:2

Goal posters and vision boards are the key to keeping my vision in front of me in all the places that count. I encourage you to write your goals in pen and then write the deadline in pencil. Sometimes you might miss your deadline to accomplish a goal, but when that happens, simply erase the date and write a new one. Missing a deadline doesn't mean you've failed—as long as you're closer to accomplishing your goal than the day you first wrote it down. I stole this major life hack—writing down my goals and posting them—from my dad. Thanks to him, this practice has rocked my world and transformed many of my dreams into reality. At eighteen, when I set out to become the youngest senior director in my company, I posted my goals. Several friends who saw them thought I was nuts.

At first, I was embarrassed when they made fun of me. But that's when I decided to own my goals! I'd had enough. I was sick and tired of those who had never accomplished squat poking fun at me. *To heck with their snide comments,* I thought. Fulfilling my God-given destiny was far more important to me than getting sucked down by the dream stealers. Take my advice: don't try to fit in when you were born to stand out. Today, I'm so glad I stuck to my guns. I smashed through my goal of becoming a senior director as a teenager and blazed a trail for Generation Y!

Don't try so hard to fit in when you were born to stand out.

67

When I achieved my goal, I felt like a rock star. The CEO of my company flew to Minnesota and presented me with the keys to my new white diamond Cadillac CTS. I was showered with flowers onstage. They asked me to speak at the national convention to thousands of the company's top performers. People grabbed me in the hallway and drilled me on how I did it. Numerous leaders asked me to share my insights and wisdom on countless conference calls and trainings for their teams. It was quite the rush for a nineteen-year-old who was crazy enough to believe she could shatter the glass ceiling and break records. That experience showed me the power of not just having a goal but writing it down.

You too can shatter records. You can smash through glass ceilings. But you've got to stop listening to your critics. Own your goals and write them down. Put your head down. And get after your goals.

SET A BIG GOAL, CRUSH IT, THEN GO BIGGER

Next, I set my sights on becoming the youngest executive director in the twenty-five-year history of the company. I worked hard and became fiercely focused. But I missed becoming the youngest executive director when I passed my twenty-first birthday. Was I bummed? Sure, for a minute. But not a month. I did become the youngest *female* executive director in the history of the company. So, at twenty-two, I shattered the glass ceiling for young women and inspired many to their dreams in the process.

Even though I didn't hit the precise goal I'd written down, by thinking big, I made my dream my reality. Even if you sometimes miss the deadline, you can ultimately achieve the goal. It's easy to beat yourself up or become tempted to give up when you miss a goal's deadline. Don't go there, sister. Stick to your goal. Just update your deadline. You've got this.

I remember as a little girl sneaking into an awards gala, joining my parents onstage in front of thousands of marketing executives as they won the prestigious President's Club Award, earning a $100,000 trip of a lifetime. My dad had posted that goal twelve months prior, even though when he posted it, he didn't really believe it was possible. He later told me that every day he saw that goal, it became a little more believable. Finally, after a few months, he fully believed it, and he and my mom turned on beast mode and went to work.

That day on the stage changed my life. At ten, I stood there in my little green sundress, elated for my parents, looking out over that ginormous crowd. I promised myself that one day I would win that very award and encourage others to live their dreams as my parents had. I thought to myself, *One day I will stand in front of thousands of people, winning big awards.* That day I began to develop a whole new philosophy. I told myself that one day, I would inspire masses. One day, I would change the course of countless people's lives, giving them hope that their dreams are possible.

That "one day" transformed into a reality at twenty-seven. I had posted a goal on my vision board to achieve entry into the President's Club of my organization by twenty-eight. I gave myself two years to accomplish the goal. The President's Club honors the top fourteen businesses in North America and rewards them with a seven-day trip to an exotic location with both the president and CEO. I was determined to empower and equip the Lady Bosses I was coaching to reach higher heights than they'd ever dreamed possible. I knew being part of the President's Club would raise the bar yet again, and serve as example for my tribe about fiercely focusing on goals. I knew I needed to prepare relentlessly to create the momentum it takes to go all the way.

So day after day, week after week, I kept mastering the mundane. I executed the IPAs (income-producing activities) every damn day. I kept powering through. I continued visualizing what it would feel like to walk across stage. I knew it would ignite the fire in my team to win that award. The promise of that exhilarating feeling kept me completely engaged.

Then, an e-mail popped into my inbox that completely blew me away. Without even realizing it, I'd snuck into the Top 40, placing me in the running for the President's Club a full year earlier than my original goal! Out of three hundred thousand marketing representatives, I had sliced through to compete with the most elite leaders in North America.

Seriously, me? I thought. I had a hard time believing it, honestly, but I put my head down and focused like never be-

69

fore. As I'd seen my parents do when I was a child, I went into full beast mode.

When a rare opportunity arises to achieve something great, seize it. Take the pen and begin to write your ultimate Lady Boss story. The pages are blank, just waiting for you to take it to the next level. Dare to change the course of your life forever.

Faced with this goal, my mantra became, "Work like everything depends on me, and pray like everything depends on God!" My team and I ended the contest period strong. Strong enough to win the award? We wouldn't know until the final convention night at the big awards gala. But I knew I'd done everything in my power to win it. As I flew off to the largest convention in the history of the company, my mind was spinning. Did this Lady Boss really have a shot against the big boys?

That day came, Saturday, May 14, 2016. I love the awards gala banquet—it's one of the largest gatherings of type A personalities on the planet! People are dressed to the hilt; the women look so glamorous in their gorgeous evening gowns, and the guys look amazing in their tuxes. As I entered the awards gala that night, my nerves were getting the best of me. The banquet hall was buzzing with electricity and excitement. As the event kicked off, I took a deep breath and prayed for the peace that transcends all understanding. I'd done everything I could and worked as hard as I possibly could. It wasn't up to me anymore—something very hard for a type A personality to accept! As I look back on the dinner, I don't remember eating anything or even what was on the menu. The management team started calling award after award. I was hooting and hollering for the winners.

Finally, the premiere moment of the company's entire year arrived. It was time to announce the prestigious President's Club! I looked at the top twenty-eight contenders listed in the gala program, and the competition was intense. Of the twenty-eight, they would only pick fourteen. The list was the who's who of the greatest producers in our company, many of whom were my heroes, my role models, my mentors—the legends in the company. I glanced again at the program to double check. Yep, my name was still listed there.

The president and the national VP of the company stood confidently at the podium. The anticipation in the banquet hall was so thick you could've cut it with a knife. My heart was racing. They started by announcing the number one position and worked their way down to the fourteenth position. When my name wasn't called in the top ten, doubt began to creep in. Maybe it wasn't my year. It was no big deal, because I wasn't planning on winning it until the next year anyway. The top twenty-eight was a huge accomplishment, and I gave it my best shot and worked hard with my team. My paychecks had grown exponentially. We'd changed more lives that year than ever before. We were blessed.

Suddenly, I was jolted back to the present. "Winning the eleventh position, from the great state of Minnesota . . . Stefanie Peters!"

I was stunned. Shocked. Elated. Dozens of emotions flooded me at once.

People were hugging me, high-fiving me. Some wouldn't let go. I couldn't catch my breath. Others, who couldn't get near me, were yelling accolades. I could hear the president calling for me to come onstage with the rest, but I couldn't break away. The crowd was surging around me. Tears streamed down my face. I brushed them back. I didn't want my mascara to run. (This Lady Boss needs to look good for the photo op!)

I finally broke away and started my long walk up the runway to join those already onstage. I was in complete shock. The roar of the crowd was deafening. I could feel the

71

hot stage lights beating down on me. The music was blaring. Cameras were in my face. I glanced at the huge screen, and at first I thought I saw a little ten-year-old girl in a green sundress. I did a double take. I glanced again—now I saw that girl was actually a lady in a teal princess dress, walking confidently up the runway. It was me.

I gave the CEO a huge bear hug. His wife placed a beautiful set of white and purple leis around my neck. I was handed a gorgeous crystal award with my name engraved on it. It weighed a ton. I couldn't stop thinking, *This just happened . . . it actually happened.*

This story represents the magic in goal setting. All of heaven moves when you set a goal and focus every day. Resources, people, and finance begin to come your way from places you never anticipated at the start.

GET YOUR GOAL GAME ON!

Want to accomplish something great? Set a goal! Want to change your life? Set a goal! Want to change your finances? Set a goal! And post them. I don't have much hope for people who refuse to post their goals. Put your goals where you can see them every day. You may not believe a word of them when you first post them, but research shows that your subconscious mind accepts them immediately. Then one day you look at them and your conscious mind believes every word.

I want to see my goals front and center so that losing focus is not an option. I post my goals on my bathroom mirror, on my refrigerator, on my television, and in my car. I then take a picture of that goal poster and add it to the screensaver on my computer and phone. Some people may say that's a bit obsessive, but those people tend to be the same people who are also mindlessly living life on default, never making progress. So I guess I'm okay with seeming a little "obsessive" to them.

Your goal posting can start out as simple as putting a sticky note on your refrigerator. You can perfect the goal later—just get it up there! Then, when you have time, jazz it up. Get creative! I print mine on a piece of paper and include a picture of myself. The picture draws my eye to my goals so I look at them more frequently.

Why don't you put this book down right now, write out a goal, and post it immediately? It doesn't have to be your biggest or best goal. But post one now; it'll make you feel good because you're getting started. And you know what they say about getting started? Getting started is half done!

I'd recommend posting your goals in two or three areas around your house and where you work. When you're tempted to get sidetracked, a goal poster in front of you is hard to ignore. Goal posters are also the perfect remedy for shiny-object syndrome. A note on your computer that says, "I call five prospects every week," is the perfect wake-up call when you're researching a random idea on Pinterest.

After you set small goals, set goals that are so big you need God's help to fulfill them. I believe God will give you a dream a size too big so you have to grow to achieve it. But that's the beauty in the journey. The person you become on the way to the goal is exponentially more important than the goal itself. Your goals have to make you stretch. They've got to take you out of your comfort zone. They've got to take you toward your dreams. Be the type of Lady Boss that, when your feet hit the floor each morning, the enemy says, "Oh crap, she's up!" Be a force to be reckoned with!

73

Lady Boss Life Hack:

People get rewarded in public for what they've practiced for years in private! Show me an "overnight" success, and I'll show you a person who's paid the price for years (maybe decades) behind the scenes when they were a "nobody." Don't be fooled—those overnight successes don't have anything you don't have!

LADY BOSS
BOLD MOVES

*(Use hashtag #UnleashYourLadyBoss
to keep us up to date on your Lady Boss wins!)*

❧ ———————————— ❧

1. Create your goal poster. Take a picture and send it to me at stefanie@unleashyourladyboss.com. I want to see it!

2. Post your goal poster somewhere in your house where you'll see it daily! This will keep you mentally engaged and propel you toward your goal.

3. Post your goal poster where you tend to get distracted. Time stealers are all around us, but if we have triggers to keep us on track, we'll get to our goal more quickly. For example: post your goal poster on your television so you'll think twice about watching Netflix all Saturday afternoon!

75

LADY BOSS
ACTION STEPS
AND AHA'S

76

IGNITE FEARLESS FOCUS

#Blissipline

"People think focus means saying yes to the thing you've got to focus on. But that's not what it means at all. It means saying no to the hundred other good ideas that there are. You have to pick carefully. I'm actually as proud of the things we haven't done as the things I have done. Innovation is saying no to 1,000 things."

—Steve Jobs

You have the same number of hours in the day as Beyoncé. That's right—you and Queen Bey are on a level playing field when it comes to time. So why are some of us wildly successful and productive while others can't seem to break out of the rut? The reason is simple: some of us are intentional and proactive about our goals, while others skate through life reacting to what life hands them. It all goes back to the choice of living life either by design or by default.

Let me explain.

Many people think "busy" means "productive." For example, I was coaching a gal—let's call her Jane—who had an aggressive business goal she wanted to reach by the end of the year. As I crunched the numbers, I found that if Jane kept going at her same pace, she likely wasn't going to reach her goal. As her coach, I owed it to her to lay out her options. Basically, Jane had two choices: step up her pace *or* adjust her deadline.

Simple. As I discussed her goals and options, it became clear that Jane didn't want to adjust her goal but admitted to not having more time in her schedule for the things she would need to do to land where she wanted. So I told her to walk me through each day of her week so we could try to find more time to focus on moving her forward. I thought, *Of course we can make this work!* As Jane and I pored over her schedule, commitments, and obligations, it was clear her life was jam-packed. She was indeed busy. But as we moved from thing to thing on her calendar, I kept asking, "Is this something you want to do, or is this something you feel obligated to do? Is this propelling your main goal forward?"

Her answer stunned me.

"Stefanie, I need to do *all* these things on my to-do list," she said. Wow. In that moment, it occurred to me that Jane was doing many of her tasks just so she could feel important. Her to-do list was holding her hostage! Right away I challenged her not to seek validation in a task, but to know her value in God and not get disillusioned or sidetracked by menial things that don't matter. By the end of the conversation, she agreed to take a number of tasks off her to-do list, like serving lunch every day at her children's school (even though she barely saw her kids during that time) and playing golf every Monday night. She also scheduled "power hours" (more on that in a bit) so she could propel her life forward!

CHOOSE INTENTIONAL LIVING DAILY

I believe some of us need to take a bulldozer to our schedules. Our schedules are often the thing keeping us from focusing on our bigger picture. We're too busy to go after our goals and make our dreams reality. Some of us are going to die with our best music still within, unheard. When we become caretakers for everyone else and never take time to be caretakers for ourselves, we're losing in the long run.

Lady Boss, no is a valid answer. And don't feel the need to explain yourself. You've got to say no to the good to have time for the great. We can always add things back to our schedule, but for now, we need to be fiercely focused if we want to win. The reality is that you can be tangled in a busy blitz with your latte in one hand and smartphone in the other without being productive at all. Being crazy busy doesn't mean you're moving your vision forward, though it probably does mean you're driving yourself up the wall!

So how do you avoid the crazy-busy myth? How do you rock your productivity when your time is limited and your dreams are limitless? The answer: learn the difference between your long-term goals and the pure busyness of life.

Most people (the people who live by default rather than design) fill their space with the urgent and sometimes unimportant instead of building space for long-term goals. Your long-term goals require space, and when you're constantly immersed in e-mails, phone calls, social media, and coffee dates (all examples of time stealers), your goals for the long-term are taken over by the urgent. At the end of the day, you're frustrated that you didn't work on your important things.

The long-term goals—for example, becoming a paid national speaker, working from the beach for three months every year, launching a global brand, starting a nonprofit—can't be cultivated in five minutes here and there. Nope.

79

Long-term goals need dedicated *time*. Uninterrupted *time*. Reserved *time*. And *space*. And more *time*. Blissipline, ladies! And time stealers, while satisfying in the short-term, often hijack your time and space. They can also zap the energy and focus you need to conquer your long-term goals.

If your cell phone rings while you're in the middle of a long-term goals project, don't answer it. Keep your eye on the prize, girlfriend. A wrong-fit referral wants to "pick your brain" over coffee? Politely decline with an invitation to meet at an engagement already on your calendar, or refer the contact to another professional. And if you're a victim of Internet rabbit hole syndrome, turn off your wi-fi when you need to concentrate. Start saying no to the good so you can say yes to the great!

Lady Boss Life Hack:

*Before adding another thing to your plate, ask yourself,
"Is this a good thing or a God thing? Is this propelling
my purpose forward?*

Don't fear removing things
from your calendar.
Fear investing in things that
never really mattered in the
first place. #JustSayNo

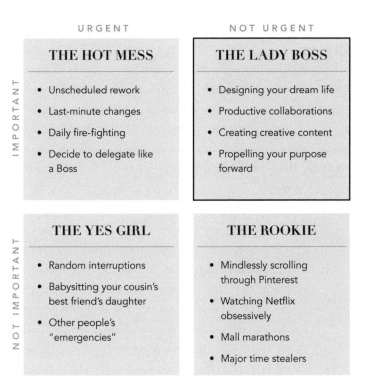

	URGENT	NOT URGENT
IMPORTANT	**THE HOT MESS** • Unscheduled rework • Last-minute changes • Daily fire-fighting • Decide to delegate like a Boss	**THE LADY BOSS** • Designing your dream life • Productive collaborations • Creating creative content • Propelling your purpose forward
NOT IMPORTANT	**THE YES GIRL** • Random interruptions • Babysitting your cousin's best friend's daughter • Other people's "emergencies"	**THE ROOKIE** • Mindlessly scrolling through Pinterest • Watching Netflix obsessively • Mall marathons • Major time stealers

81

POWER HOURS AND A DREAM ROUTINE (DR)

What I'm about to say will probably irritate a few folks. Hopefully, you'll thank me later. One of the strategies you're probably using to get all your day-to-day responsibilities done is multitasking. And personally, I'm not a fan. The reason is that multitasking—a gift many of my fellow Lady Bosses possess—is actually the very practice that is draining us.

It's really difficult to power through to the next level of your vision when you have too many balls in the air. I get it—you're a mom, a wife, one busy gal, or all of the above. But you're probably exhausted from saying yes to everything and taking care of everybody, all while trying to run the world!

So what's the answer? It's easier to have a fresh sense of focus when you have a dream routine, or DR. Your DR sets your mind in the right place from the moment your feet touch the floor. With a DR, you become a force, the fabulous master of your day instead of a robot on autopilot pulled in a million different directions. Instead of impulsively checking your e-mail when you wake up (which leads to putting out fire after fire), your DR will create a consistent routine that works for you.

My morning DR looks something like this:

1. Practice devotions, gratitude journaling, and prayer.
2. Exercise while listening to personal development programs by way of podcasts or the Audible app on my phone. (My personal favorites are Joel and Victoria Osteen, Lewis Howes, Darren Hardy, Joyce Meyer, Brian Tracy, Zig Ziglar, and Jim Rohn.)
3. Drink green protein smoothie and take vitamins.

After your DR, implement power hours. Power hours are forty-five minutes of uninterrupted time to laser-focus on one of your long-term goals, plus fifteen minutes of rest. They are a must if you want to get to the next level. During your power hours, you're building, innovating, creating, and designing something major, or using that time to grow or brainstorm your game plan with intention. Only after your DR and power hour should you begin your daily fire extinguishing. (Note: It's important that you find a DR and power hour method that works for you. I suggest the DR and power hour in the morning, but if you know you're a night person, consider having this time come later in the day or evening.)

As research shows in the spectacular *Huffington Post* article "Give Your Brain a Break" by Jenny Dearborn, your brain can only focus on a task for about forty-five minutes until your productivity plummets and your attention inevitably travels elsewhere. Duh! That impulse to check Facebook or grab a snack in the middle of a task is because your brain needs a break. The problem is that we don't have a game plan with breaks built in. That's why I created the power hour for myself. Use a timer if you need one, and decide in advance not to allow any distractions. Period. Unless your work space catches fire, you're in Lady Boss Fierce Focus mode.

For me, I optimally like to conduct at least two power hours a day to complement my three nonnegotiable goals for the week. It ensures that I make progress daily on what I know I need to get done—no ifs, ands, or putting a goal on the backburner. This practice takes crazy discipline. But you know what? Discipline is the key to becoming successful.

> You've got two options: choose the pain of discipline or the pain of regret. And I've found that discipline weighs ounces, while regret weighs tons.

POWER PARTNERS UNITE

Another crucial way to keep yourself fiercely focused and your feet to the fire is finding a power partner. Goals, power hours, and a DR are superb. But even with all this Lady Boss ammo in your arsenal, a fellow go-getter in your corner challenging you regularly and checking in on your progress is one of the most fabulous strategies for crossing the finish line.

One of my good friends, Stacy, called me and said, "I'm sick of being overweight, and I look at you and I want to be healthier. What would you recommend?" I told her my truth and shared how running was one of the keys to my healthy lifestyle, and I challenged her to run a half marathon with me.

She responded, "I can't run a mile, let alone thirteen!"

I said, "Hey girl, wait a minute, you asked *me* for advice! There's no way you can keep doing what you're doing and expect different results. I will team up and be your power partner, and we'll keep each other accountable. I'll lay out a training program so you can work up to our half marathon. And I will run it with you! Are you game?"

She reluctantly agreed. She was scared but desperate to lose the weight. So we started small and added more to our workout day by day. We had twelve weeks to prepare, so I laid out the training schedule and told her we would text each other every day after finishing. At first, Stacy wasn't thrilled, but she also had a goal in mind she wanted to reach. Day after day, she told me it was tough to get started, but she felt lit up that she was finally making progress. Some call it the "runner's high." We promised each other we wouldn't miss one day on the running schedule, and I stressed to her that this was a nonnegotiable goal. Excuses? Not an option.

On one particular day, the rain and wind woke me up before my alarm. I knew this particular day was packed and that the only time I'd be able to run was early in the morning. Any other morning, if I'd been the only one responsible for holding myself accountable, there's no way I would've forced myself to get out of my warm, comfy bed to run in the rain. But I knew I couldn't let Stacy down. I put on my big-girl panties and got out there and ran.

Was it pleasant? Nope. But as soon as I was done, I ran in and texted Stacy some encouragement and checked in to let her know I ran my miles. To my surprise, she had run hers too! She told me she would never have put in the miles that day if it weren't for me.

Long story short, Stacy and I ran the entire half marathon, she lost thirty pounds, and she's since fallen in love with running. I saw her at church recently, and she informed me that she's training for a triathlon! It's so amazing to be a single piece of a larger puzzle, helping people succeed—especially with good friends. Also, it was super rewarding to see Stacy get the results she was looking for. I felt like a proud mama at the finish line. I believe the biggest reason she got the results she wanted was because we teamed up, set goals, and kept each other's feet to the fire. We focused together.

Sometimes having a power partner (or accountability buddy) to keep you accountable to your goals is the difference between "get 'er done" and "someday." It's so easy to let life get in the way, followed by getting too busy, which immediately leads to getting sidetracked. But our greater purpose depends on our focus and discipline. Without focus, our results aren't what they should be. So the moral of this story is to find a power partner to ignite your inner Lady Boss and keep that flame going strong!

85

LADY BOSS
BOLD MOVES

*(Use hashtag #UnleashYourLadyBoss
to keep us up to date on your Lady Boss wins!)*

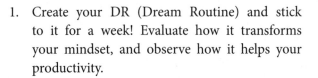

1. Create your DR (Dream Routine) and stick to it for a week! Evaluate how it transforms your mindset, and observe how it helps your productivity.

2. Take out your calendar and schedule two power hours this week. Challenge yourself to see how much you can accomplish in these first two sessions.

3. Pick your power partner, define a goal, choose a daily check-in time, and stick to it for thirty days.

LADY BOSS
ACTION STEPS
AND AHA'S

87

FAIL FAST
AND FURIOUS

#FeeltheFearDoItAnyways
#ExcuseTheLongHashtag

"Think like a queen. A queen is not afraid to fail. Failure is another stepping-stone to greatness."

— Oprah Winfrey

At the beginning of my career, I wanted everything perfect. I wanted to shine like the true Lady Boss I was meant to be. But I made the mistake of becoming consumed by the ideals of how I wanted to be rather than embracing who I already was. Over time, I became paralyzed. I couldn't make any moves unless they were "perfect" (queue Beyoncé's "Flawless"). I had to not only be a Lady Boss but a Super Lady Boss who did everything perfectly, all without breaking a sweat.

You can imagine how much I got done in those early days . . . not much. Then something clicked when I read *Failing Forward* by the amazing John C. Maxwell. Talk about a life changer! I felt as if I finally had permission to fall flat on my face and still come out a champion in the end. His advice helped take the pressure off, and it gave me not only the freedom to fail but also a sense of urgency to fail fast.

I learned that if I failed fast, I could figure out what worked and what didn't so I could reach my goals more quickly. Listen up, ladies! Failure is absolutely necessary. You'll never achieve success without a lot of failure. Lady Bosses need failures as stepping-stones to success. The more failures I experience, the more success I have. In my early days, when learning to run my business, I had to fail. That was part of the deal, because if I wasn't failing, I wasn't trying enough new things. At the end of the day, when you're not failing, you're not playing a big enough game. You're being way too cautious.

SOMETIMES YOU WIN, SOMETIMES YOU LEARN

I get it; failure sucks. Who doesn't hate failing? But if you want success, fail fast and fail hard. One of Maxwell's most recent books is *Sometimes You Win, Sometimes You Learn*. I love this title. Yes, we all want to win. We have our vision, our game plan, and we're hustling to make big things happen and happen *now*. But sometimes—no, most times—things don't go as planned. Someone gets upset and won't return your phone call. You're drowning in drama. A client relationship goes south. A goal isn't met. You might reach a goal only to discover it was the wrong goal.

These experiences can be disheartening. You'll begin questioning yourself. But wait. Stop. Just don't go there, sister. Always remember, the only way to lose is to not learn from your "failures." Sometimes you win, sometimes you learn. You don't lose if you choose to learn.

"When your goal is to gain experience, perspective, and knowledge, failure is no longer a possibility."
—Sophia Amoruso, author of #*GIRLBOSS* and founder of Nasty Gal

When I started my business at age eighteen, I failed more times than I can count. I had to learn to communicate with people better, network, strategize, and speak in public. The list of things I had to work at was long.

Small children fail thousands of times in a single day. They fall down, they spill things (sometimes on purpose), they goofily try and fail all day long. The more babies try and fail, the more fun they seem to have figuring out how to rebound, all while feeling good about themselves in the process. When was the last time you did that? Why is it that as full-grown women we have one small failure and are tempted to lie down and die? I've seen women get one loud no in their business and quit that same day! Lady Boss, don't fall into this trap. A no is not the end. A mistake is often a sign to up the ante and push harder. A bad day sets the bar to rock it out tomorrow.

"When we give ourselves permission to fail, we, at the same time, give ourselves permission to excel."
—Eloise Ristad

FEEL THE FEAR
AND FAIL (FORWARD)

The reason failure is a big, fat, scary problem for a Lady Boss is because of one awful word: *fear*. When a door slams in our face, we're consumed with what we did wrong. We never want to go through that again, so we obsess and analyze every setback until we're paralyzed. Fear and failure go hand in hand. That's why we don't get back out there after we fall down. But to live our dreams, we have to dig deeper than what feels comfortable. That means we can't take no for an answer. The only way to lose is to quit.

As a teenager, I considered myself quite the introvert. If I had the choice to go to a party or stay home with popcorn and a movie with my bestie, you better believe I was choosing the latter. Putting myself out there wasn't easy. I was too nervous to take risks. But I quickly learned that everything I wanted meant pushing past my comfort zone. So when one of my mentors recommended I attend a morning networking event, which required getting up at the crack of dawn and fighting rush-hour traffic to meet strangers, I wasn't thrilled—the idea was far from my definition of fun—but I reluctantly agreed that going would be a good way to expand my network. I could feel the anxiety in the pit of my stomach and couldn't deny the voice in my head screaming, *Don't do this. You won't know what to say! What will people think about you? What if there's awkward silence?*

The what ifs yelled louder and louder. But then I heard it—a clear, reassuring whisper: *Feel the fear and do it anyway.* So I put my big-girl panties on, and I headed to the networking event, bound and determined to put myself out there. I decided that I'd apply tools I'd learned from a Dale Carnegie course I'd taken in the past; I decided to start a conversation using the FORM approach, where you ask about family, occupation, recreation, and mission.

91

So there I am. It's 7:00 a.m. and I'm all dressed up, with no prior business experience. But I'm ready to mingle and network like I'm running for governor. I head straight to the front table, ready to activate Operation FORM Approach. I've got this in the bag!

I spot the check-in table with three guys sitting there. The first guy at the table kindly greets me with, "Good morning. My name is Danny. How are you on this fine day?"

I reply with enthusiasm, "Great, Danny! Are you married?"

Dead, awkward silence.

Yep, nailed it. Except I'm pretty sure that is not what good ole Dale Carnegie meant when he said to begin a conversation asking about one's family. *Oh my gosh*, I think. *You didn't just ask that! Yep. Sure did.* Danny's eyes immediately get big. This introvert feels like she's dying inside, and I'm sure I'm probably turning every shade of red imaginable. I long to disappear. But, to make matters worse, Danny—clearly embarrassed—looks at the guy next to him and uncomfortably says, "I am married, but my friend Bob isn't . . ."

"Oh, great. Nice to meet you!" I say, trying to save face before promptly excusing myself. A mad dash to the restroom is definitely in order. I saw that moment going wildly different in my head. I'd failed miserably at what I'd set out to do. As I'm in the restroom, I try my best to calm down. I tell myself that I will never see those guys again. I mean, the Twin Cities is huge, right? Not so much, and no such luck, ladies. I'm not kidding when I say that I saw Danny and Bob twice more in the next month at other events. The Man Upstairs definitely needed a little comic relief—or perhaps was testing me to see how far I was willing to push myself to pursue my dreams.

Reflecting on that day later in the evening, I thought about the upside of that catastrophe. As poorly as I had done, I figured that at least I couldn't get worse at networking. I could only go up from there. I share this story to say this:

when you start something new, prepare for the bumps. And trust me when I tell you that fear comes with the territory. It just does. But a Lady Boss doesn't let fear boss her around. She tells fear who's boss, and then she keeps moving forward.

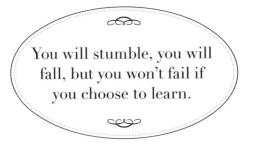

You will stumble, you will fall, but you won't fail if you choose to learn.

LEARN FROM LOSING

In sports, you can learn more by losing than by winning. When my team lost a basketball game, I would replay every scenario in my head that lead to that outcome—every rebound I didn't get, every shot I missed. I would rack my brain for ways to improve my performance.

I love this quote from Michael Jordan, arguably the best player in the history of basketball:

"I've missed more than nine thousand shots in my career. I've lost almost three hundred games. Twenty-six times, I've been trusted to take the game-winning shot and missed. I've failed over and over and over again in my life. And that is why I succeed."

I believe it's the same in life. Anything worth doing is worth doing poorly at first. At the start of most new things, you're going to suck. Then, after you suck for a good amount of time, you'll graduate to average. But remember, nobody celebrates average. Nobody wants to go to an average dinner followed by an average movie. We want to enjoy an amazing dinner and experience a phenomenal movie with a hot date.

If you keep learning and practicing, you'll eventually become incredible at your craft.

So many people, when they see a successful person, see the bright lights, fame, followers, fans, and fortune. They don't see the thousands of hours of hard work, repetition, mastering the mundane, disciplining the disappointments, and failures.

94

"Giving up on your goal because of one setback is like slashing your other three tires because you got one flat."
—Unknown

Malcolm Gladwell, author of the book *Outliers*, among other bestsellers, studied the lives of extremely successful people to find out how they achieved success. In his research, he found that no "naturally gifted" people emerged. Instead, he found a direct statistical relationship between hours of practice and achievement. No shortcuts, no naturals.

Bill and Paul dropped out of college to form a company. They spent thousands of hours practicing computer programming before anyone ever heard about them. Gladwell found these two boys had become addicted to programming and spent about 10,000 hours on it before they launched their company in 1975. Now everyone has heard of Bill Gates,

Paul Allen, and their company, Microsoft. They're two of the richest people in America.

Full circle update: I now consider myself an extroverted introvert who has absolutely fallen in love with networking! But first, I had to find my style to make it work. I had to learn from my failure and strategize a game plan. So instead of believing the lie that I wasn't a good networker, I deliberately changed my thinking. I created my own "power principles." This made a huge difference, and as a bonus, I fell in love with networking.

Here's the cheat sheet I created of my power principles:

1. Be a "FUN" networker: When I network, I am a fearless unstoppable networker. My tip: enjoy it!

2. Don't go just to go: I always ask myself if I'm passionate about the event. If the answer is no, I don't go. Life is too short to spend time in places that aren't purposeful. Go to places that light you up. If you would regret missing an event if you skipped it, go.

95

My early networking failure helped me put failure in general in perspective. It helped me understand that while many view failure as the end, it's not. In fact, a failure is often the start of something spectacular. Lady Boss, expect to fail. And when you do, resist the urge to beat yourself up. Have fun, and consider your failures a gift. Every Lady Boss, from Arianna Huffington (founder of *Huffington Post*) to Joyce Meyer (world-renowned evangelist) to Tina Fey (comedic goddess), has "failed." The Fail Fast and Furious club is one all Lady Bosses join, whether we like it or not.

*"Rock bottom became the solid
foundation on which I rebuilt my life."*
—J. K. Rowling

SOMETIMES, YOUR BEST ASSET IS WHAT YOU DON'T KNOW

Sara Blakely, who's a huge business crush of mine, has one of the most inspiring failure comeback stories of all time. As a successful door-to-door fax machine and office supplies salesperson, she knew a thing or two about uncomfortable undergarments and hosiery. She recounts her father asking her every single evening at dinner, "How did you fail today?" And she carried that with her as she had several career setbacks, including failing the law school entrance exam, the LSATs, twice!

Sara decided becoming a lawyer wasn't in the cards, but she had a great idea. When she met with a patent attorney to protect her idea, the attorney thought her idea was so bad he asked if he was on *Candid Camera* and laughed her out of the office. Sara didn't care. She wasn't about to let some haughty attorney steal her dream. So she decided to write her own damn patent. She went on to become the youngest female self-made billionaire by taking $5,000 in savings and transforming it into a $250-million-a-year company called Spanx. She grew her undergarment empire without any outside investment, debt, or even a cent spent on traditional advertising.

When she created Spanx (otherwise known as a woman's best friend) she'd tapped into a huge niche in the intimate apparel market, and it paid off. She became the first self-made female billionaire in the U.S. But her road to success was long and not without several stops and starts. In a CNBC interview, she shared, "The fact that I had never taken a business class, had no training, didn't know how retail worked [is why] I wasn't as intimidated as I should have been." How fantastic is that? Her lack of knowledge is why she was gutsy. She had no idea what she didn't know. "What you don't know can become your greatest asset if you'll let it and if you have the confidence to say, 'I'm going to do it anyway, even though I haven't been taught or somebody hasn't shown me the way,'" she said.

Imagine if Oprah had said "forget it" at age twenty-two, after being fired from her first television job and told she was "unfit for TV." Who would've blamed her? But if she had given in, not only would the world be lacking serious hope and joy (thanks, Oprah!), but the universe-altering empowerment revolution Oprah ignited wouldn't have happened. Don't let a setback set you back; let it set you up for comeback.

97

LADY BOSS
BOLD MOVES

(Use hashtag #UnleashYourLadyBoss
to keep us up to date on your Lady Boss wins!)

1. Journal a recent failure and recall the lessons you learned from it. Make the decision not to stew. And for goodness' sake, avoid a pity party at all costs! List three ways you intend to turn your failure into a win for your playbook.

2. Encourage another Lady Boss you know is struggling with failure. Remind her that you only fail if you quit. Suggest a baby step she can take right now to keep herself moving forward.

3. Create a Fail Forward Action Plan. What are you going to do to rebound from your recent failure? Who in your tribe can help you bridge the gap? What can you do right now to meaningfully move forward?

LADY BOSS
ACTION STEPS
AND AHA'S

99

MASTER YOUR MINDSET

#GoPro

"Success is not to be pursued; it is to be attracted by the person you become."
—Jim Rohn

Almost all leaders have one thing in common: they've spent years working to become the best version of themselves. While others are playing, these leaders are sharpening their saw. While others "Netflix and chill," these leaders spend their valuable time reading self-development books, attending personal growth seminars, and investing in their most valuable asset: themselves. I call it personal development.

In his book *The Seven Habits of Highly Effective People*, Stephen Covey talks about sharpening the saw. He uses the analogy of a woodcutter who is sawing for several days straight but becoming less and less productive. The process of cutting dulls the blade. The solution? Sharpen the saw.

According to Covey's website, stephencovey.com, sharpening the saw means preserving and enhancing the greatest asset you have: you. It means having a balanced program for self-renewal in four areas:

Physical: *Beneficial eating, exercising, and resting*

Social/Emotional: *Making social and meaningful connections with others*

Mental: *Learning, reading, writing, and teaching*

Spiritual: *Spending time in nature, expanding spiritual self through meditation, music, art, prayer, or service*

Lady Boss, if you want to experience your ultimate life, keep growing. What are you doing today to change your life for tomorrow?

GROW, RUN, REFLECT, REPEAT

The more I study my favorite leaders and reflect on my life, the more I discover how important personal development is. If you're committed to maximizing your potential and making a serious impact in the world, you need to push yourself. You can't just will yourself to become a Lady Boss. Change is hard, and overcoming negative habits is even harder.

101

Most people walk blindly through life, never discovering their gifts or developing their talents. To claim all you're capable of *and* experience that euphoric feeling of powering through whatever is holding you back, you have to master your mindset. When you work on your mind with intention, you'll immediately feel victorious.

The first step in mastering your mindset is to evaluate where you are in life, then gather tools to step up your game. As you've likely figured out, I'm a huge fan of podcasts, books, and consistent physical activity. After you've done your self-assessment, go a step further. Every morning, before your feet even hit the floor, read five pages of your favorite life-affirming book. This one simple action will make all the difference in the flow of your day and your attitude as you move from thing to thing. If reading doesn't work for you, try praying or simply setting an intention for the day.

I like to ask myself regularly: What am I missing? How can I sharpen my skills? What's one thing I can do today to help my team play at a higher level?

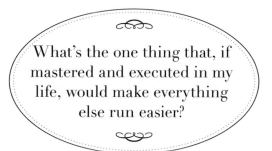

What's the one thing that, if mastered and executed in my life, would make everything else run easier?

This intentional exercise alone keeps me laser-focused, but it also reminds my psyche that to do better, I have to think better. Lady Boss, think on purpose. Fill your mind with positive affirmations and affirming beliefs about yourself and your dreams. It's also crucial to become the master of your emotions. Your brain needs nourishment like the rest of your body. Keeping doubt, worry, fear, and anxiety at bay can become a full-time job if you're not strengthening your mind every day.

HEART WORK BEFORE HARD WORK

In all my years of coaching, I've found there are two types of people: chasers and attractors. Let me ask you: are you attracting success or are you chasing it?

I used to be one of those people who chased success. Early in my career, I found myself exhausted *and* unfulfilled. I was beating my head against a wall chasing what I thought was success. I'd set my goals the first day of the month and hustle

102

until I felt like I wanted to pass out. Did I gain traction? Sure I did. But did I feel like something was missing? Without a doubt!

Don't get me wrong, I believe hard work and hustle can overcome serious stagnation and get you where you want to go. But the drawback is that you may burn yourself out in the process. And let's keep it real—it's hard to sustain a nonstop, hundred-mile-per-hour hustle. Of course, I broke records and blazed a trail early in my career. But honestly, you can lose everything you've worked hard for in a hot second if you aren't playing *your* authentic game while trying to claw your way to the top.

Yes, hard work is essential to achieving whatever goal you set for yourself, but hustle and hard work need to collaborate with *heart* if you truly want to pursue your higher purpose and build your legacy.

About five years into my career, I had a trying situation that almost took me down for the count. Business was booming. I was leading a team that seemed unstoppable. We were kicking butt and taking names, and I felt like I was on top of the world. Then, out of nowhere, one of my best friends and business partners turned his back on me. He just walked away. As you can imagine, I was devastated. I felt broken, crushed, and like a knife was twisted in my stomach. I didn't want to get out of bed. What was the point? I felt lifeless.

That was one of the darkest times in my life. This person was my best friend, and now he wanted nothing to do with me. I felt completely rejected. Day after day, I asked myself who I was. I didn't seem to know or even care. This went on for what seemed an eternity. Then one day, I woke up and thought, *This is ridiculous. I'm letting this guy control my days and thoughts, and ultimately I'm letting him occupy valuable real estate in my head rent free. Nope. No more. He is stripping me of my destiny, and I'm over it.* John C. Maxwell says:

103

"1. Not everyone will take the journey.
2. Not everyone should take the journey.
3. Not everyone can take the journey."
—John C. Maxwell

Lady Boss, you've got to learn to let people go! Bless and release! Someday they may come back into your life, but until then, stop thinking about them. It paralyzes you. It's a complete waste of time. God has far greater relationships for you in the future. But if you keep holding on to past relationships, you'll miss the new people completely.

I didn't recover overnight, and it was incredibly difficult to let the entire matter go. But eventually, I was tired of feeling drained. I knew it was my time to move on and draw a line in the drying cement. I wasn't going to let him dictate my destiny. Ruminating on what happened compromised my ability to focus, visualize, and attract my blessings.

I decided to do some major soul-searching first. I needed to get to the heart of why I do what I do. In years past, I'd operated with the mindset of "whatever it takes, no matter what!" But that mentality took me down, hard and strong. And yes, I created "success," but I realized after digging deep that I had built much of my success on a foundation of sand. I knew what I was doing but not why I was doing it. I had the hustle without the heart.

So I went back to the drawing board. And like I said, it didn't happen right away, but I started to combine *hard work* with *heart*. Even though, at first, my team didn't grow as fast as before, we were now building on a solid foundation. I started training differently and leading from a place of leadership and love versus pure bottom line.

Soon the culture changed, and the environment started to feel authentic and real. Our clients could be who they really were and get the answers they needed instead of being inundated with information and the same canned responses. Once we started making these course corrections, things started to heat up again, but this time it didn't seem exhausting. Now, things seemed to flow.

TURN ADVERSITY INTO ADVANTAGE

We weren't "hunting" success, we were unleashing it. When we changed, things fell into place, and people started coming to us. I wasn't only feeling success; now, I was feeling significance. Man, what a feeling! Even though the loss of a friendship took me to dark depths, it forced me to reevaluate my life, my business, and my mindset. When I made heart (and mind) changes, the transformation led to peace, joy, gratitude, and victory. One of my darkest hours turned into one of the best life-changing events of my life. That experience led me to lead from the heart. Looking back, I'm thankful God allowed me to go through that. Today, my mantra is:

105

Different than I expected, but better than I imagined.

From that event, a seed was planted. I knew I was made to make an impact on the masses with a message of inspiration and hope. Now it was just a matter of time. I knew that mastering my mindset would require a different prescription, which included being consistent with what God put in my path, trusting His ordained plan, and being diligent day-to-day.

Fast-forward to a year later. I met an incredible woman, Allison, whom I now consider one of my best friends. I coached her for a year, and we forged a beautiful friendship. Little did I know that this friendship would turn into a life-altering partnership. We cofounded Lady Boss Empire, an empowerment platform and community for women. I cannot tell you how jazzed I am that God brought us together.

"Every adversity, every failure, every heartache carries with it the seed of an equal or greater benefit."

—Napoleon Hill

To unleash the opportunities that exist in your life right now, regularly challenge yourself with these pivotal questions:

1. What is the one thing that, if mastered, would make everything else I do easier or unnecessary?
2. How can I become an expert in my industry or profession?
3. How can I increase my service?
4. There are always better ways to do what I'm presently doing. What are they?
5. How will my work be performed twenty years from now?
6. Everything in the world is in a state of evolution and improvement. How can I become an innovator in my field?

As you build your empire, you'll need to break away from the average way of thinking. Force yourself from this day forward to think outside the box. Keep in mind that it's easy to operate on autopilot, but if you can force yourself to think through things and create systems, you'll be on the brink of a breakthrough. Think about the CEOs, game changers, pioneers, trailblazers, and bosses you respect. They live and breathe the cutting edge. It's time to take creative and innovative thinking to the next level.

Start by disrupting your normal routines that aren't using your innovative juices. If something doesn't push your limits, scrap it, sister! When you do the same thing over and over again without self-assessment, you get the same results. Let's dare to elevate our lives and decide to up our A-game.

FIXED MINDSET VERSUS GROWTH MINDSET

I recently attended a leadership summit where one of the speakers asked a question that rocked my world: "What's the one thing in your business that, if mastered, would make many of the other tasks you do regularly unnecessary?" My answers: embracing technology and branding my business.

Eeeeek, I thought. I even quivered at the thought of jumping into the unknown. Let's be honest: I'm known to be a paper-planner-and-pen kind of girl. The thought of venturing into the world of virtual systems made my knees week. I was under serious attack. I mean, where the heck is that "cloud"? And what if I do it wrong? What happens if I embrace technology and my life becomes less efficient and more complicated? What if I waste tons of time *and* I'm thrown off track?

Then the speaker said something else that completely stopped me in my tracks. He said,

"Stop thinking about the fear of the unknown. I want you to force yourself to think about what you could potentially gain if you mastered this! Command your mind to think about this as an exciting new adventure, then dream about the possibilities. Embrace the unknown!"

So I flew back home, felt the fear, but decided I'd conquer my goals of leveraging technology better and branding my business. First, I hired a graphic designer and social media consultant. Then, I set my mind on taking my brand to the next level. Even though I was quite uncomfortable the whole way through, in a weird way, I felt empowered. When fear would grab hold of me, I'd take a step back and say, "I don't need to have it all figured out, but I will do what I need to do today to move my vision forward and grow my brand." I decided that slow progress was better than no progress.

Fast-forward to today—now 80 percent of our business comes from social media. We stepped up our game and it worked. I'm so grateful I made the plunge. The return on investment has been astounding! As a Lady Boss, I've learned that one of our biggest mistakes as business owners is allowing stagnation to set in. Growing your life, business, and team on purpose is a daily activity. You've got to innovate. What worked last year will not continue to work year after year. We live in a world where our cheese is constantly moving. We have a choice to either be shocked by the shot of the stun gun or anticipate it. We need to become innovative so we never get caught asking who moved our cheese.

But to be real with you, my mindset is what truly made it possible to venture into uncharted territory and up my technology and social media game. I chose to have a growth mindset instead of a fixed mindset. Listen up, ladies: in your life and business, there will come moments—possibly daily—when you'll decide which mindset you're going to bring to the table. You can choose a growth mindset of abundance, positivity, and expansion, or you can choose a fixed mindset rooted in limitations.

A fixed mindset replays thoughts like, *I hate numbers and have never been good at math. I don't want to grow too big or too fast because I'd never be able to manage that kind of growth. I'm going to go with the cheaper option just in case something bad happens,* and the list goes on. The ladies who rest on their own hype often shatter to pieces when failures and setbacks knock them down.

A fixed mindset can be suicide for the dreams and goals of a Lady Boss. We've got to change our mindset to acknowledge that nothing is permanent. Everything is up for negotiation and discussion. When it comes down to it, your possibilities and future are greater than both your limiting beliefs and your natural brilliance. If you find yourself knee-deep in self-talk about how your past is holding you back, how a lack of resources is keeping you stuck, or how you're as successful as you're ever going to be, you need a major mind makeover.

> The only thing standing between you and your goal is the BS story you keep telling yourself as to why you can't achieve it.

When you adopt a growth mindset, you're thankful for challenges. You rejoice at the opportunity to learn and to become wiser and more agile. You know there's always room to improve, and you know there's no limit to your potential. I appreciate the transparency from actress Kate Winslet, who confided, "I'd wake up in the morning before going off to a shoot and think, 'I can't do this; I'm a fraud.'" After reading this, I had an epiphany. If a talented Hollywood royal like Kate Winslet questions herself before going to work, we Lady Bosses have to choose to keep pursuing our dream every day we wake up. We can't expect confidence and a growth mindset to magically appear. We have to put it on like we do the rest of our fabulous outfit.

When we master a growth mindset, we choose to move on instead of dwelling on our shortcomings. A growth mindset embraces change, lets go of the past, celebrates others' successes, and thrives in uncomfortable circumstances. These thought patterns are within our reach, but we have to work at thinking this way. We have to decide on purpose to push, fight, and call ourselves out when we default to fixed-mindset thinking. And when in doubt, refer to one of my favorite scriptures: "Do not conform to the pattern of this world, but be transformed by the renewing of your mind" (Romans 12:2).

LADY BOSS
BOLD MOVES

*(Use hashtag #UnleashYourLadyBoss
to keep us up to date on your Lady Boss wins!)*

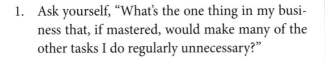

1. Ask yourself, "What's the one thing in my business that, if mastered, would make many of the other tasks I do regularly unnecessary?"

2. After you identify your answer from question 1, take one step in the next twenty-four hours to move toward mastering your one thing.

3. What daily ritual can you add that will help you keep choosing your dream over default? For example, I say a prayer of gratitude every morning when I wake up. This is my time to thank God for a new day and new opportunity to pursue the vision in my heart.

111

LADY BOSS
ACTION STEPS
AND AHA'S

BUILD YOUR DREAM TRIBE

#LadyBossesWhoSlayTogetherStayTogether

---

*"Be strong, be fearless, be beautiful.
And believe that anything is
possible when you have the right
people there to support you."*

—Misty Copeland

113

If you'd met me ten years ago, you would've met a girl who didn't get teamwork. I used to get frustrated if someone wasn't just like me. If someone wasn't type-A and driven in the same ways I was, I had zero patience.

At the beginning of my career, I went completely rogue. I naively put my head down and powered through my tasks. From the outset, I definitely "got 'er done." But something was missing. Things weren't working out as I had planned, and worse, the feeling of fulfillment wasn't there. After going down this path for months, I became even more frustrated and disillusioned. When I took a step back and reevaluated what I wanted, where I was going, and the people I wanted to align myself with, I knew something wasn't right.

I'd already shifted my mindset and overcome many of my fears and doubts. I'd even developed a clear vision of where I wanted to go. But still, I knew something was off. After forced soul-searching and prayer, the message came through that I needed a tribe . . . and fast. The realization hit me like a ton of bricks. With a tribe, a motivated team, we would go further faster. A tribe would help push me beyond my comfort zone. I could be a missing puzzle piece for them and add value to their lives. It would be a win-win.

When you're building your ultimate Lady Boss life, you'll learn fast that your tribe is the magic. When I look back at the past three years, everything from business advancements, the President's Club, and personal development transformation within myself and team directly correlates to the Lady Boss tribe we've been fervently building.

If there's one thing I've learned, it's this: The validation you seek won't always come from those in your inner circle.

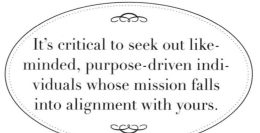

It's critical to seek out like-minded, purpose-driven individuals whose mission falls into alignment with yours.

As you inch closer to the life you've always dreamed of building, you'll realize that your tribe is the missing link . . . they are the individuals who energize, motivate, push you, and ultimately validate all you're running after.

Look at your goals, past, present, and future. Where do you want to be in the next year, five years, or even ten years?

Be intentional when selecting your tribe. Diversity is key. When you have a dynamic mixture of people from all walks of life, you'll find that each person comes to the table with different strengths. As a collective, these strengths are magnified, and your team is able to accomplish exponentially more than any one person on their own.

"One can chase a thousand, and two shall put ten thousand to flight."
—Joshua 23:10

John C. Maxwell says it best: "You may be good, but you are not *that* good!" If you want to go fast, go alone. But if you want to go far, go together! If you keep doing what you're doing, you'll keep getting what you're getting. So it's your choice, a choice that often separates the women from the girls. We can isolate and try to make it happen on our own. Or we can collectively come together and collaborate with a tribe of positive friends, partners, coaches, and mentors to crush it.

115

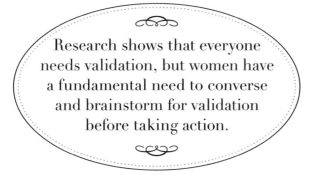

Research shows that everyone needs validation, but women have a fundamental need to converse and brainstorm for validation before taking action.

DESIGN YOUR DREAM TEAM LAB

Thomas Edison, when asked why he had a team of twenty-one assistants, responded, "If I could solve all the problems myself, I would." Edison created the "teamwork" laboratory because he understood the power of a team and knew he would be light-years ahead of the pack if he could get the most innovative minds working together synergistically. Edison's laboratory team concept is the basis for most of our current laboratories and research development centers today. While he didn't invent teamwork, he was one of the first to make it popular.

Sarah Miller Caldicott, Thomas Edison's great-grand-niece, once said, "He viewed collaboration as the beating heart of his laboratories, a sustaining resource that fueled the knowledge assets of his sprawling innovation empire." And just think—of Edison's 1,093 US patents, many are still in use today.

Starting strong is great, but finishing strong writes the history books. I believe having a strong tribe and teaming up is the difference between success and significance.

Write down what your ultimate tribe looks like. Are you lacking sales savvy? Financial prowess? Do you need a good referral partner? What about a prayer partner or workout buddy? Your tribe isn't all about business all the time. Your tribe is poised to bolster your life goals, and that includes the whole shebang: family, spiritual, creative, and financial goals. And that's why it's crucial that you remove toxic folks from the mix. Yep, I'm going there. Lady Bosses, if you want to go after your life's next chapter in a major way, you need to evaluate the people who are influencing you, and vice versa.

As John Wooden says, "Show me your friends, and I'll show you your future!" When gearing up for your dream team, clear out the debris (the folks who don't belong) to make room for the treasure that awaits. My advice for you:

if you want to set your life on fire, seek those who fan the flames, not douse the spark!

Use these five key Lady Boss questions to assess if someone is adding value or holding you back from your destiny:

1. Does this person have a vision or philosophy about life and/or business that inspires me?
2. Does this person have a next-level goal they're actively working toward?
3. Is this person strong in an area where I'm weak and want to improve?
4. Is this person authentic and relatable?
5. Does this person persevere and push through tough circumstances, or do they allow life to dictate their attitude, dreams, and potential?

If asking these questions leaves you feeling positive about someone, continue to cultivate your relationship. That person belongs in your tribe! But if the answers to these questions leave you feeling anxious, nervous, or unsure about someone, you may need to reevaluate if they belong in your life.

Your vision is too precious and important to be sniped out by energy-suckers. Energy-suckers include people with negative attitudes and people who are complacent or apathetic. If they're sleepwalking through life, maybe they shouldn't be in your tribe! Invest in people who deserve your time. Lady Boss, don't waste the days you have left putting out fires and jumping over Drama Divas. If you remember nothing else, remember that you're a combination of your five closest friends, the books you read, and the places you discover. Choose wisely.

117

*A tribe that builds together
blooms together.*

BUILD YOUR TRIBE,
AND YOUR TRIBE BUILDS YOU

Within my tribe, I have four core teams that help me perform at my peak. I call them my Fabulous Four. They include my Access Team, Accountability Team, Advisor Team, and Advocate Team.

ACCESS TEAM (AKA MENTORS/
GURUS IN YOUR FIELD)

This team ignites your fire, stimulates you to think bigger, and challenges your status quo. These catalysts are fifty thousand feet in front of you, teaching you how to cultivate your creativity and catapult you into the next level of your business and life. I call them the Access Team because they empower you to access your greatness by challenging your thinking and pushing you to rise higher. Your Access Team inspires you to take your next bold move!

When you implement what you learn from these leaders, the sky's the limit on what you can accomplish. Listen to podcasts, read blogs, listen to audiobooks, watch online videos, and so on. If you're the smartest person in the room, you're in the wrong room! Make a list of five people you want on your Access Team. Make sure you set up a game plan to bring them into your life and connect with them regularly. Questions you want to ask your Access Team include: What experience in your life or business forced you to take a next-level risk? What are my blind spots? What advice are you glad you listened to? What advice are you glad you didn't listen to?

If you're the smartest one in the room, you're in the wrong room!

ACCOUNTABILITY TEAM (AKA YOUR POWER PARTNERS)

Ideally, members of your Accountability Team are at about the same level as or a bit in front of you (as far as your career goes). It works great if it's a two-way street, meaning they keep you accountable to your goals and you do the same for them. With your Accountability Team, you need to ask: Who will keep my feet to the fire and challenge me to be my best every day? Who will hold me accountable to what I say I'm going to do even when the emotion of what I'm feeling has left me?

My mother and I work closely together and talk every Tuesday at 9:00 a.m. We check in to make sure our goals are on point, course correct along the way, and help each other navigate our respective journeys so we can focus on the true tasks at hand and power through them. I love what Proverbs 27:17 says:

119

Iron sharpens iron, as one person sharpens another.

Feelings will fail you, but a strong Accountability Team will help you power through the difficult days so you get the results you're looking to achieve.

ADVISOR TEAM

As your empire grows, you'll need to become a master at leveraging your time. You'll need to outsource aspects of your business if you want to scale, enjoy the journey, and remain big-picture oriented. Your Advisor Team should include any or all of the following: CPA, bookkeeper, personal assistant, financial advisor, business lawyer, insurance broker, personal stylist, social media consultant, business coach, intern, housekeeper, meal prepper, therapist, pastor or spiritual advisor, prayer or meditation partner, nanny, and personal trainer.

Your Advisor Team helps you optimize your week, month, and year so you can work smarter in the areas you're strongest. Yes, you're a crazy-talented Lady Boss. You may feel like you can do it all, and I have no doubt you can, but the real question isn't *can* you do it but *should* you do it?

Lady Boss Life Hack:

*Delegate, delegate, delegate! Stick with your
Strength Zone, and leverage your time by becoming a
master delegator!*

You can clean your home; be the full-time chauffeur for your family; cook all the meals; manage your Twitter, Instagram, Facebook, and LinkedIn profiles; update your website; manage your books; make the best financial decisions without help; and run your business. But ask yourself an important question: Would you feel balanced or stressed if you controlled *all* aspects of your life? Your Advisor Team doesn't just help you avoid burnout; they help you save money and time.

ADVOCATE TEAM

Your Advocate Team consists of the people you're adding value to within your organization or business, including your employees, mentees, team, and interns. This team offers the opportunity to become the ultimate coach and game-changer in someone else's life. Priceless.

These are the people whom you invest in without the expectation of receiving anything in return. I'm a huge believer in the principle of sowing and reaping. Meaning, what you sow, you shall reap. But regardless of that principle, the feeling of pouring into someone selflessly is fulfilling and life-giving.

I volunteer at MN Adult and Teen Challenge, which is a faith-based drug and alcohol rehabilitation center. It's been so gratifying investing in the lives of women who are on the road to recovery. It's amazing to see the sparkle in their eye return as they regain the hope that their circumstances are not the end but the beginning of a whole new chapter. It doesn't get better than witnessing women rewrite their stories to reach their ultimate destiny. To know I've played a small role in that journey brings me to tears when I think about it. When you hear the testimonies of redemption at graduation, you know you're in the right spot!

I also love investing in my Lady Boss Empire tribe and seeing the growth they experience as I coach and empower them with the resources and confidence to shine their true greatness. Case in point: in the early days, one of the leaders of Lady Boss Empire expressed frustration at not having passion or purpose. She wanted to do more and be more but couldn't quite grasp how to break out of her rut. Together

121

we worked to start her own business and transition from working full time to becoming a stay-at-home mom who offices from home and runs her business passionately. But above and beyond that, she's thankful for the Lady Boss leadership principles.

"Becoming financially free and running my own business trumps it all!" she recently said. "I am not the same girl I was!" It's astounding to watch the growth of women who decide that now is their time and they're done making excuses.

In the end, you can build your tribe however your heart desires, but I like to make sure I'm investing in leaders instead of followers. As a Lady Boss, you've been called to lead a legacy. Your empire is the stuff of legend. When you lead followers, at best, you gain more followers. But when you rise up and lead, collaborate with, and inspire other leaders, you never quite grasp the lasting impact you'll truly have in the world. #LeadYourLeagcy

LADY BOSS
BOLD MOVES

(Use hashtag #UnleashYourLadyBoss
to keep us up to date on your Lady Boss wins!)

❧ ———————— ❧

1. Get a coach. I'm a huge fan of hiring people who challenge me and my ways of thinking.

2. Clear the debris and create your Tribe Wish List. Start dismantling the toxic, ineffective, and emotionally draining relationships from your life. Then make a list of who you need to add to your tribe based on things that are missing from your life. Find people you need in the areas of finance, emotional support, spiritual fulfillment, health, and business goals.

3. Build your Fabulous Core Four teams. In a day planner (either online or on paper), start filling seats! Keeping a record of who is in your tribe is important, because over time, these seats might evolve, change, shrink, or grow. To know where you're going, it's important to know where you've been and who's helped you get there!

Extra Credit: Take a fellow Lady Boss under your wing and start breathing belief into her. For example, take her out to lunch, send her an inspirational message or quote, or simply tell her what a phenomenal person she is! It will not only potentially change the trajectory of her life, but you'll feel pretty fabulous as well!

123

LADY BOSS
ACTION STEPS
AND AHA'S

BECOME A LEGEND AND LEAVE YOUR LEGACY

#SecretSauce

"Lady Bosses that leave a legacy don't see a seed; they see the tree, and then they envision the forest!"

—Stefanie Peters

"Call 911! We need help and we need help NOW!" screamed my mother.

It was a cold, musty, dreary day in late October, and I was passed out cold. I was sixteen, a junior in high school, and had been preparing for the most important varsity cross-country meet of my running career. Since I'd been asthmatic all my life and struggled with allergies, I knew in the back of my mind that running on the golf course that particular day could be lethal.

The four-kilometer (2.5 mile) course was extremely wet from recent rain. I found out later that the grounds crew had just sprayed the course with a ton of chemicals. When I arrived at the meet and began my warm-up, I began struggling to breath. I compensated by using my inhaler, popping a Sudafed, and inhaling several steroids to keep my symptoms at bay. I was determined to run this critical race at optimal performance. But things felt off. When my mother arrived, she insisted I take my nebulizer. I did, and right away my body started to shake.

"Feel the fear and do it anyway," I kept telling myself.

So I stepped up to the starting line after the warm-up and got in the zone as much as I could under the circumstances. I looked down the long starting line and saw the top seven varsity runners from over twenty schools. Some of the best female runners in the state were there.

The starting gun cracked, and off we went. *Focus and forget about the peripherals,* I kept telling myself. *Fight through it! Get after it, girl!* Something felt really wrong, but I kept telling my mind to ignore it.

My dad yelled to encourage me to kick it up at the one-mile marker. He was timing me. I was almost on pace for a personal record. That gave me hope, so I dug deeper and tried to give it everything I had. But then something shifted. I felt like I was kicking it into high gear, but my steps were slowing, and my time was getting farther off. I felt confused and disoriented. But I kept going.

As I passed the two-mile marker, my dad yelled to drive harder. By then, I was significantly off pace. But I couldn't understand why. I thought I was leaving it all on the course! I felt my heart beginning to race, and my breathing was deteriorating. This was a crucial race for me to qualify for State. What was my deal? I was so confused!

I thought the finish line was in sight, finally! *Where have you been all my life?* I thought. I had to run through the shoot, and then I would be finished! The world started to spin. I vaguely remember hearing my dad yell, "Keep going!

What are you doing? You've got to finish the race! Get in the shoot!" Wait, what? Hadn't I already crossed the finish line and gone through the shoot?

I have absolutely no recollection of what happened in the next five minutes.

My dad told me I never finished the most important cross-country race of my life. He says I staggered eerily over to a post in the finish-line shoot and rested my head on top of it. Dozens of other runners ran by me. Dad yelled again, "You haven't crossed the finish line, you've got twenty yards to go!" More runners passed me. My dad, sensing I was about to pass out, grabbed me and said, "Come on, Sissy. Let's walk it off." My heart was racing way too fast, and my breathing was out of control.

He told me later that as we walked, my lips and body began to turn blue. As he looked at me, my eyes rolled toward the back of my head. I collapsed, and he sat me on the ground and screamed for help. Someone finally found my mom.

I hazily remember being carried by four cross-country runners to the medical tent, but no one was there. Someone yelled that the trainer had gone to the clubhouse. There is almost always an ambulance at cross-country races, but not at this one. Meanwhile, time was ticking and nobody knew how much time I had left.

As they sat me down in the clubhouse, my heart seemed to race even faster, and it got harder to breathe. The trainer yelled for everyone except critical personnel to clear the room. What was happening?

The trainer whispered to my mom and dad, "We've got to get her heart rate down right now or it could stop altogether." *What?! Am I dying?* I thought.

At this point, I felt my heart rate climb to an all-time high I had never experienced. The room began to spin again, and I started to shake. A knife could've cut the heaviness in the

127

room. Not only was my mom crying, but my dad was crying too. They were sure they were watching their daughter die in front of them. The trainer stared at me and my mom with a look of terror.

Suddenly I had this unexplainable peace rush over me. It felt like I was in a fight for my life, yet I also felt like I was seeing the room from above. I was having an out-of-body experience. I looked down and there I was, in front of the trainer, gasping for air.

The serenity I felt is still surreal when I reminisce about that day. I was enveloped by tranquility and complete trust and calm in God. I was at peace.

I started to speak but could still see the situation from above. Then I looked straight at my mom and said, "It's okay. Don't worry. I'm going to be okay." Then I looked at the trainer with absolute clarity, and said, "No matter if I stay or if I go, I know Jesus Christ is my personal Lord and Savior. So no matter what happens, it's all going to be okay." By now my mom was absolutely sobbing, realizing she was losing her baby girl. My dad was in complete shock and disbelief, feeling completely helpless.

But once those words came out of my mouth, I could sense my heart rate beginning to normalize. My breathing began to slow. Color came back into my lips and face.

I'll spare you the details of the recovery process, but what I will say is that my body wasn't used to the amount of drugs being pumped into me, so it started to react violently. But once my body got to the point of stabilization, I sat in complete shock at what had happened. Once I got my bearings, I slowly limped to the car. I felt like a weak, elderly woman, exhausted from that horrendous experience.

THE PARADIGM SHIFT FROM SUCCESS TO SIGNIFICANCE

I sank into the seat of my car, still wracked with pain from the convulsions. Yet my thoughts were crystal clear. I suddenly saw my life from a new perspective. I told my parents, "I've been totally chasing the wrong goals. The cross-country titles I've relentlessly pursued, the four-point grade point average, the varsity letterman's jacket, National Honor Society, now seem so hollow. Mom and Dad, what truly matters is my relationship with God and how I make an impact in people's lives. I really can't take much else with me when I die."

As I think back on the day I almost lost my life, I am in awe and astounded at how God turned a near-death experience into a complete paradigm shift—one that I needed if I was going to fulfill the purpose He placed in my heart. As horrid as the experience was, I'm so grateful and humbled that He allowed me to stay here and to gain the insight I did. Honestly, that is exactly what this stubborn German girl needed to shake her up and show her the light.

Many of us wonder about the spiritual purpose for our lives. Why are we here? What is our purpose? My near-death experience gave me the perspective to ask God the big questions in life, and to realize how fleeting it all is. Without having gone through it, I might never have realized the true strength of my spirit and the fragility of my body, of the *human* body—we are so temporary but so powerful when we harness our God-given gifts and purpose.

Have *you* truly examined your talents, passions, and who you were created to be? I've found that no matter where we are in life, the resources, connections, and strength to do what we're called to do will be provided to us. But sister, God can't steer a parked car. We have to take action.

Once you've tasted significance, success will never completely satisfy you. What type of legacy are you leaving? If our dreams only impact us, then we need to check our priorities. What is our grander purpose? How do we want to be remembered?

When we do our part with the gifts we're given, doors will open that no man, woman, or situation can shut! And when we continue to use what we're given, we are given infinitely more in return. Call me crazy, but I believe we are spiritual beings having a human experience. (Stick with me here—I promise I'm not jumping off the deep end. To live your ultimate purpose you need to hear this.) I personally believe that our ultimate power source is God. If we unplug and don't connect with our spiritual selves, we quickly lose heart, become complacent, and lose our way. Life becomes tasteless and our fire dies.

Until I made God the CEO of my business and life, I was working hard but lacked the focus and purpose only He can bring. Before God was the center of my business, I felt like the driver with no idea where I was going. When someone pointed out that I was going in the wrong direction, I replied, "But I'm making great time!" People, businesses, and life will sometimes fail us, but God never will.

This point was made even clearer to me recently. I was reading a book called *Fervent* by Priscilla Shirer, and this passage in Key #6 was life changing. It reads:

> *If I were your enemy, I'd magnify your fears, making them appear insurmountable, intimidating you with enough worries until avoiding them becomes your driving motivation. I would use anxiety to cripple you,*

to paralyze you, leaving you indecisive, clinging to safety and sameness, always on the defensive because of what might happen. When you hear the word faith, all I'd want you to hear is "unnecessary risk."

I've coached hundreds of Lady Bosses through the years, and I believe the number one reason women slam on their breaks and stop pursuing their passion is because of this loathsome thing called fear. We fear the unknown, we fear what people will think, and we fear that we don't have what it takes.

Perhaps your fearful thoughts sound something like this: *What if I can't do it? What if pursuing my destiny is a total waste of my time and energy? I'm not ready. I don't think I have what it takes to make my dream a reality. Better to be safe than sorry.*

But, here's the deal. We have two options: 1) we can become paralyzed by fear and stop moving forward, or 2) we can step out in faith, feel the fear, and get after it, regardless of our feelings.

P.S. PLAYING IT SAFE NEVER WRITES THE HISTORY BOOKS!

It's time to get fed up with our fear and to get over it. Our minds play stupid, lethal tricks on us, and fear is a frontline weapon that cripples us Lady Bosses. But that is precisely what faith is for. When our fears tell us we can't, faith is designed to remind us that we can and we must!

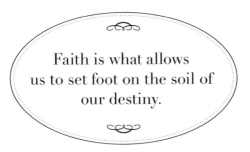

Faith is what allows us to set foot on the soil of our destiny.

Extraordinary legacies never happen by accident. When we're caught in the grind of making a living, not only can we forget this, but we forget that our lives are meant to be designed around the legacies we were created to leave behind.

Think about your life in the past year. Were you truly *living* your life, or were you barely existing? My Lady Boss challenge to you: Don't read your life or write your life. Become the intentional *best-selling* author of the amazing story you've always dreamed. Lady Boss, how do you want to be remembered? It's up to you!

Make TODAY
Your Masterpiece

CARRYING IT FORWARD

I cofounded Lady Boss Empire, an empowerment platform and resource center, to equip women to live the life of their dreams. I was enjoying being a marketing rep for the Inc. 500 company I've partnered with since 2007, but I wanted to make an even bigger impact on a larger scale in women's lives.

One of my fellow Lady Bosses asked me early on, "Why are you working so hard? You've already accomplished many of the goals you set out to achieve."

I told her, "It's not about me anymore. It's about the lives we touch and how we can change the trajectory of people's destiny."

I believe that when our purpose transcends a paycheck and rises to meet our God-given mission, our true greatness can fully bloom.

Paying it forward keeps me up at night. Ever notice how you can count the number of seeds in an apple, but you can't count the number of apples in a seed? Your job is not to convince someone to bloom where they are planted. Your job is to plant seeds and nurture them by watering and placing them in the most optimal environment to see those seeds truly flourish.

"The two most important days in your life are the day you are born and the day you find out why."

—Mark Twain

LEAVE YOUR PAST BEHIND AND LEAD YOUR LEGACY

I love to read stories of legendary men and women. Most of the time, I don't have to dig far into their lives to see the investment of time and energy from mentors who equipped them to rewrite history and literally change the world as we know it. I believe this is who we are meant to be. We are mentors and coaches, empowering others just like others have empowered us on our journey. When you equip future movement makers to win, you win. We all win.

One of my favorite living legends is the famed Christian evangelist, author, and speaker Joyce Meyer. Her life story is proof of how we can turn the most destructive of circumstances into a mighty and powerful victory. Joyce, who was repeatedly molested by her father from a young age until she was a teenager, turned her horrific past into a triumphant message about hope, forgiveness, and compassion. Of her childhood, she shared, "At school I pretended I had a normal life, but I felt lonely all the time and different from everyone else. I never felt like I fit in."

Can you imagine growing up feeling such loneliness and despair? Can you imagine the vision and tenacity it would take to overcome such adversity? Joyce is a hero (or should I say,"shero"?) in my book because she decided not to become defined by her adversities and to instead become a beacon of light and vehicle for hope for millions in the world. Today, her ministry spans the globe, her books have lit up the *New York Times* best-seller list, and for thirty years, her annual conferences have attracted more than two hundred thousand women. Even more, Joyce frequently shares her story of overcoming abuse and the transformational power of forgiveness. Joyce didn't allow her history, fears, or family to keep her from living her destiny and impacting millions of people. I absolutely adore this quote from Joyce and couldn't agree with her more:

> *"No matter what has happened to you in the past or what is going on in your life right now, it has no power to keep you from having an amazingly good future if you will walk by faith in God."*
> —Joyce Meyer

Joyce isn't any different from you or me. We all have the opportunity to change our story at any time. She's a walking testimony of how God can use anything for our good and for the good of others.

My challenge to you: decide that every day from this day forward you'll push through fear, dance through doubt, and own your story (good or bad) for the betterment of this world. People need to hear your story. Your destiny belongs to you and no one else, Lady Boss. When you're no longer on the planet, the spirit of your purpose will still be here, touching lives and sprinkling blessings over those left behind. Whether you think about it or not, your life's message has a song to sing. Make sure you take the time while you can to make it a song we remember.

YOUR LIFE, YOUR STORY, YOUR PEN

Rule #1 of becoming a legendary Lady Boss: when writing the story of your life, don't let anybody else hold the pen. Your spouse, parents, friends, and coworkers don't get to shape how you want to be remembered. They don't get to decide your life. You do! You have the opportunity, right now, to write your ultimate life story. Design your story to be a page-turning best seller filled with triumph over defeat, joy over sorrow, peace over conflict, love over hate, and courage over fear. You deserve that life. You're building your empire, not because you want fame or fortune, but because you were created to change lives, inspire others to follow their dreams, and impact the world in a major way. Below are seven game-changing ideas for you to write your life anew:

1. Start a personal development program.
2. Attend a dynamic church.
3. Begin to pay down your debt.
4. Launch your blog.
5. Kick off your business.
6. Start your own YouTube channel.
7. Take the first step on that project that's been pulling at your heart for years.

135

Today is the only day you have to start the life you've always dreamed. You don't have to do everything on your list, but you have to start somewhere. Do something. Stop procrastinating. Choose purpose over perfection, rise up, and beat the game of fear. We are born for such a time as this.

There you have it, Lady Boss. It's time to take massive action toward your destiny . . . and right now. It's time to leave your mark. A Lady Boss's vision is much bigger than one that can be accomplished by a single person. When we all dare to come together to do the "impossible," we become legends. We crush the status quo and illuminate the legacy of possibility for generations. If you've been praying for a sign, this is it. Step up and lead the Lady Boss Revolution.

I dare you to join the movement! #UnleashYourLadyBoss

LADY BOSS
BOLD MOVES

*(Use hashtag #UnleashYourLadyBoss
to keep us up to date on your Lady Boss wins!)*

1. Create three pillars for your Lady Boss Playbook for Success and share it with another woman you believe is destined for greatness. My dear friend, business mentor, and second cousin, Eric Worre, taught me his playbook for success, and I still practice it to this day:
    *   Say yes
    *   Tell the world
    *   Figure it out

2. Fast-forward ten years into the future and write your bio. What are your accomplishments? How are you impacting others? What legacy are you designing to leave behind?

3. Go to unleashyourladyboss.com/powerplan, print off the full PDF, and fill it out completely. Take time to reflect on your life, lessons learned, and how you want to live and lead your life from here on out! It's *your* time to lead *your* legacy!

Extra Credit: I want to see your progress and cheer you on! Post on social media and tag me @ladyboss_sp and use the #UnleashYourLadyBoss hashtag!

137

LADY BOSS
ACTION STEPS
AND AHA'S

138

DEAR LADY BOSS,

You are equipped and ready to unleash your Lady Boss within! You have the ten keys to unlock your ultimate life and ignite your greatness. Now it's your time to take action and build the life you're fabulously, stupidly, unabashedly in love with.

When you decide to build life by design, it will be completely unnerving. Trust me, this is completely normal. You'll have amazing days, but you'll also have days you feel like you've lost your vision completely. You will question yourself. It's all okay.

The first step to getting started is to just get started! You'll find incredible mentors along the way as long as you keep trusting the process and trusting yourself. I'm a living example of the saying, "When the student is ready, the teacher appears."

Will it be hard? Heck yeah! But will it be worth it? Every damn day.

Your transformation won't happen overnight. But as you apply these principles and use this book as a resource, you will become the Lady Boss of your own life. Even in my most difficult days, I power through because I know my lifeguard walks on water! Choose resilience even in the midst of chaos. Choose to shut down the chattering in your head that whispers, *you are not enough.* In God, you are enough. He has equipped you with more than enough. The impossible is possible.

So now it's your turn to unleash your Lady Boss! I dare you to grab the pen and write your own story! #WeGotThis

Your cheerleader and fellow Lady Boss,
Stefanie Peters

ACKNOWLEDGMENTS

Wow, where do I even begin?

First things first, I want to thank my heavenly Father for placing a purpose on my heart that could not be denied. Your faithfulness through all the highs and lows of life is astounding. Thank you for putting this song in my soul and giving me the opportunity to inspire women to their higher calling. I am forever grateful.

To Julie Peters (a.k.a., Mama P.): Thank you for loving me in my darkest hours and never giving up on me. Your constant commitment and devotion is priceless. Your encouragement through life has been the catalyst to help me go for the purpose God placed on my heart. You are such an amazing mentor, incredible Proverbs: 31 Lady Boss, and the BEST FRIEND a girl could ask for! I thank God constantly that he chose you to be my mother; he gave me the best! Love you forever and always. The best is yet to come!

To my dad, Steve Peters: You never even liked running, but you ran because you knew I had a passion for it and needed a running buddy. Whether you were helping me with real estate, writing, or giving me general life advice, your guidance has been invaluable for me in becoming the person I am today. Thank you for being the true Godly example I model myself after. I LOVE you with all my heart.

To my brother, Ben Peters: Thank you for being the "salt" on my popcorn and adding flavor to my life. Your dedication to throwing impromptu jam sessions and road trips keeps me on my toes in the best ways possible. Love you, bro!

To the cofounder of Lady Boss Empire, Allison Crandall: Thank you for opening my eyes to what life is truly about. You have taught me to embrace the moment and the relationships God puts in our lives. Thank you for bringing the fun, glitz, and glamour to my life. I can always count on you to bring the party to the party. Love you, soul sister!

To Gloria Krueger, my nanny since age three: Thank you for loving me unconditionally—even with all the sass I gave you through the years. Your servant leadership and kindness will always be in my heart!

To Lady Boss Empire: My mantra has always been "blessed to be a blessing," and I have wanted to pay that forward to you. I would have never expected the joy and fulfillment each one of you has brought to my life. I am better because of you; the gifts you have brought to the table make our tribe one of excellence. I love you like a pregnant lady loves pickles!

To my "haters" and those who tried to crush my dreams: Without you I may not have made the decision to relentlessly run after the vision God put on my heart. You can't have the testimony without the test! Thanks for the challenge!

To you, reader: I am overwhelmed with all the support I have received from people like you reading this book, many whom I hold dear and many I don't know personally. My hope and prayer is that this resource gives you the inspiration you give me on a daily basis to do what I do! Thanks for inspiring me to keep on keeping on! We are in this TOGETHER!

If you want to learn more about Lady Boss Empire . . .

My heartbeat is to see you win in business and life. That's why I cofounded Lady Boss Empire, an empowerment platform to equip you to ignite your inner greatness. I'd love to connect with you and be a continual resource on your journey to success and significance. If you're looking to connect with a tribe of inspirational women where iron sharpens iron, go to our Lady Boss Facebook fan page and "like" it to get inspired on a regular basis at: Facebook.com/LBEmpire. You can also subscribe to our e-newsletter for insight and motivation at unleashyourladyboss.com or contact me directly at stefanie@unleashyourladyboss.com.

ABOUT THE AUTHOR

Stefanie Peters is a national speaker, author, and serial entrepreneur. She started her first business at the age of eighteen. She shattered the glass ceiling and became the youngest female executive in one of the fastest-growing companies in North America. Stefanie was determined to help women find financial freedom and independence. As her movement grew, she cofounded Lady Boss Empire, an empowerment platform and resource center for female entrepreneurs. Besides building multiple businesses, she is a savvy real estate investor, certified John C. Maxwell coach, avid runner, fitness competitor, and a top performer in the Miss Minnesota International Pageant. To learn more about Stefanie, visit UnleashYourLadyboss.com.

143

SCHEDULE
STEFANIE
TO SPEAK AT
YOUR NEXT EVENT!

❧ ——————————— ❧

Stefanie Peters is guaranteed to deliver an inspiring, entertaining, and life-changing message! She is a certified speaker, coached by her mentor, best-selling author John C. Maxwell. For more than a decade, Stefanie has been inspiring and teaching audiences to:

- Unlock their **inner greatness**
- **Break through** barriers and self-doubt
- Take strategic **actions** to get **results**

Through her specific strategies, power plan, and hilarious real-life stories, Stefanie ignites audiences to take their lives and businesses to the next level!

FOR MORE INFORMATION

Visit UnleashYourLadyBoss.com
or contact Stefanie directly at
Stefanie@UnleashYourLadyBoss.com.